The Little Black Book of
Business
Etiquette

Michael C. Thomsett

amacom

American Management Association

This publication is designed to provide accurate and authoritative
information in regard to the subject matter covered. It is sold with the
understanding that the publisher is not engaged in rendering legal,
accounting, or other professional service. If legal advice or other
expert assistance is required, the services of a competent professional
person should be sought.

Library of Congress Cataloging-in-Publication Data
Thomsett, Michael C.
    The little black book of business etiquette / Michael C. Thomsett.
        p. cm.
    Includes index.
    ISBN 0-8144-7754-2 (pbk.)
    1. Business etiquette.   I. Title.
HF5389.T48   1991   91-53060
395'.52—dc20   CIP

Printing number

10 9 8 7 6 5 4 3 2 1

Contents

Introduction

Never ignore a gut feeling; but never believe that it's enough on its own.

—Robert Heller

This Little Black Book explores the world of unspoken rules in your company. Its purpose is not to supply you with lists of arbitrary restrictions or guidelines but to examine conventions in a very practical way. When you are confronted with a difficult situation, how much should you say? When is it appropriate to speak out, and when should you keep ideas to yourself? How do you confront the political problems created by others? What general rules should you follow at meetings and business meals and during telephone discussions? What statements do you make by the way you dress? What is the most effective way to lodge a complaint?

Many of the rules of behavior that govern corporate life remain unspoken, even in organizations headed by enlightened, aware, and caring leaders. The corporate family, unlike the personal family, survives more on what is not said than on what is clearly stated. In a healthy family, for example, conflict between two people is confronted, discussed, and resolved. Both sides are given a chance to express their views and feelings, and the issues are discussed in both practical and emotional terms. In a corporation, however, most communications take place with both sides keenly aware of a line beyond which expressions of emotion are considered inappropriate. You do not cross that line. If you do talk about how you feel, you choose your words carefully, because emotions

1

are qualified and restricted according to the setting. You may express anger or enthusiasm, but only at a level that is acceptable within the corporate culture.

This limitation on emotional openness rules every aspect of corporate life. It controls the way a message is conveyed, and it determines how you deal with anger or with elation. If you enjoy a healthy form of expression in your personal life, you'll need to change mental and emotional gears to survive in the corporate setting.

Survivors in the corporate family develop a sense of what works and what doesn't. In this book, you will find a recurring theme: As long as your motives are right for you and your company, and as long as you deal with others from a position of truth, you cannot go wrong—assuming, of course, that you correctly choose the time and the place to have your dealings. The combination of focus and timing is what really defines how you should act and is what underlies the rules of behavior in the corporate world.

This Little Black Book raises some difficult issues and presents general guidelines for contending with them; however, you will need to develop your own sixth sense about focus and timing. To help you achieve this objective, you may rely on this Little Black Book as a personal tool for survival. It would be poor form, and perhaps bad manners, to leave this book where less enlightened members of the corporate family might find it. If your desk has a drawer with a lock, use it. If you have a file that no one else wants to read, store this book somewhere in the middle of that file. Think of this book as a personal diary, and take steps to prevent your corporate brothers and sisters from peeking at it.

1

Water Cooler Diplomacy: Setting Your Ground Rules

People are beginning to see that the first requisite to success in life is to be a good animal.

—Herbert Spencer

"How did I do in the meeting?" the anxious young manager asked his older mentor. "Did I sound professional?"

The mentor replied, "You presented yourself very well for the most part. The report was crisp and to the point. Only one thing I suggest you change. Requesting financing shouldn't be referred to as hitting on the bank."

You finally have the job you've always wanted. You are running a department, leading other people, and gaining influence with the decision makers. Even though there is a great deal of pressure, you can deal with all of it; in fact, you thrive on it. Still, one aspect of your new position puzzles you: surviving corporate politics.

The mechanical aspects of communication are not the problem; you express yourself clearly and understand the issues. Rather, the difficulty arises from questions of strategy. The truth is, sometimes you simply

3

do not know the unspoken rules that govern what happens in your company.

MYTHS AND REALITIES

Every company develops its own customs—customs usually based on the beliefs and preferences of management. No two organizations are governed by precisely the same set of customs, although the general standards are often similar from company to company. What would you do in the following situation?

> **Example:** Your company serves a traditional Monday morning breakfast that is attended by all managers and executives. The meal begins with a prayer led by the president.

Several rules, both spoken and unspoken, might affect a manager's decision on whether to attend the breakfasts. One is not to stay away from these breakfasts on religious grounds; even if no one verbalizes the rule, common sense should tell you to remain silent and tolerate the imposition of the president's religious beliefs, whether or not they are in accord with your own. Another rule is not to use too much work as an excuse for not attending; that this is poor form may be conveyed very directly and in no uncertain terms.

> **Example:** While there is no precise schedule for coffee breaks, managers generally take theirs at 10 A.M. while everyone else breaks before or after that hour.

Here, a tradition has been established. If you, as a manager, appear in the lunchroom while subordinates are on their break, you will be violating the unspoken rule that you do not take your breaks with subordinates. There may be no logical reason for it, but the fact is that the rule exists.

Both these cases reject the idea that managers can operate from simple formulas. In fact, learning and dealing with unspoken rules are probably your most challenging tasks in surviving in the corporate world. The procedures in your department, the preferred format for reports, meeting agendas, and budgets all can be reduced to writing; expectations for them are specific. Beyond that, the rules become intangible and must be perceived rather than read somewhere in an operations manual.

The beliefs we bring with us to work do not necessarily correspond to the ways things really are. Some of these beliefs are wishful thinking while others, taught to us in school, apply only in a very conceptual world. Three popular myths about custom and the unspoken rules are:

Myth 1: Popularity isn't important as long as you do your job well. The truth is, popularity is very important. In spite of work-related demands, highly competent but unpopular managers do not survive as well as their fairly competent but popular counterparts. Your wish to be popular should never affect your judgment or the way you supervise—that's a mistake many first-time leaders make—but by balancing work demands with a cooperative nature, you will gain needed allies for your progression upwards in the company.

> **Example:** One extremely able manager was passed over for promotion, even though perfectly suited for the new job. The reason: She had a reputation as a person who didn't cooperate. She was not a "team player."

Myth 2: Each person's role is clearly defined by rank and title. The belief here is that your relative position on the corporate ladder dictates how much influence you have. But even in the military, where the ranking system is highly structured, this is not always true. For example, what happens when a twenty-two-year-old lieutenant is given command over a forty-five-year-old sergeant with twenty years of experience? Usually, one of two things: Either the young lieutenant tries to make a lot of changes, gaining enemies in the process, or he and the sergeant come to an agreement as to who will take charge and over which areas. Similar compromises are made in civilian corporate life. Rank and experience do not always correspond; that's when compromises in responsibility need to be made.

> **Example:** A fairly inexperienced manager was put in charge of a department. One of the employees had many years' more expe-

rience. The new manager could have taken charge on the basis of her rank and title; instead, she recognized that some forms of authority extend beyond rank and title. She and the more experienced employee came to an agreement about areas of responsibility; to a degree, direct supervision became symbolic.

Myth 3: The rules of behavior are nothing more than common sense. Without a doubt, common sense plays a critical part in determining your overall behavior in a company environment. The problem is that often the unspoken rules not only involve little common sense but may even contradict it.

For example, many companies develop an insider's language, using terminology that has meaning only to members of the corporate family. To a newcomer, some of the terms may seem ridiculous. However, using them may be how company men or women let others know that they are dedicated to the organization. Anyone ridiculing those terms is perceived as an outsider.

Example: The CEO of a large company went by the nickname Bud. When the newly hired manager attended a meeting and proposed purchasing half a million dollars worth of capital assets, one vice-president responded, "That would require an act of Bud." Although the new manager was very amused, he knew enough to not make fun of the expression and chose to just let it pass.

CORPORATE LOYALTY

These three myths all revolve around loyalty to the company. Traditionally, dedicated company men and women believe in everything for which that company stands. They strive to be team players, which means competence as well as popularity; they respect rank and title without fail, but they also know—perhaps intuitively—where the real power and influence lie. And they go along with the unspoken rules of behavior, whatever they might be, even if that means adopting slang expressions.

There is no conflict between corporate loyalty and the need to maintain personal standards—unless company policies violate your own code of behavior. In that case, taking a stand is very important for your personal integrity, even if it explodes the rules and jeopardizes your career. Assuming that you are loyal to your company, what are the guidelines for behavior? What rules should you adopt that benefit the company directly, without violating your own code? Here are some guidelines (see also Figure 1-1):

Figure 1-1. Guidelines: company loyalty.

1. Evaluate situations with the company's goals in mind.

2. Avoid taking part in gossip and rumor.

3. Respect the chain of command.

4. Communicate with everyone who is affected by your decisions.

5. Think before you speak, then decide whether the timing is right.

6. Be aware that there are at least three agendas in every meeting.

1. *Evaluate situations with the company's goals in mind.* In attempting to define company loyalty for yourself and to act within the definition, a good place to start is to understand the company's goals. Having a clear understanding of corporate objectives can prevent confusion when you need to make decisions. It is also not unreasonable to state that the company's goals should guide your decisions. Using objectives in this way makes sense and is good management policy.

This idea assumes, of course, that your company's top management has gone to the trouble of developing and communicating goals. If it has not, then you are forced to evaluate situations in complete chaos rather than in a defined environment.

> **Example:** You are faced with a difficult decision in your department. You attempt to arrive at a solution by asking, "How will the outcome of my decision fit with the company's goals?" The problem, though, is that you aren't sure what those goals are. Attempting to use company goals as a basis for decision-making works only if you can determine management's agenda. Some companies try to set goals by developing a one-year budget; that rarely answers the question about goals.

2. *Avoid taking part in gossip and rumor.* A chronic problem in many companies, large and small, is the rumor mill. The problem is most acute in companies where communication is poor or nonexistent. However, even when management makes every effort to keep everyone informed and involved, rumors and gossip may flourish.

A good rule of behavior is to steer clear of rumor or gossip on any level. When someone approaches you with information, diplomatically suggest that nothing may be expected to come from idle talk except a decline in morale. When another person comes to you to seek verification of a rumor, ask that the employee not continue to spread it; then find out whether there is any truth behind it. If you discover that a rumor is true, make it your responsibility to ask top management to share information. Point out that the rumor is circulating; that's worse for employee morale than knowing the facts.

> **Example:** One of the employees in your department repeats a rumor he heard—that the headquarters office will be relocated in

a distant city. You encourage the employee to not repeat the rumor and then approach the vice-president of your division to learn whether the rumor is true or false and to ask management to let the employees know. The rumor is disruptive and is a symptom of a need for better communication. By handling the situation in this way, you are following the rule of etiquette.

3. *Respect the chain of command.* Any information should go from your subordinates through you to your boss. Avoid breaking the chain of command; it exists to preserve order.

Also be aware of the invisible chain of command. Some people do not hold rank and title but do have influence in the company. Respect that chain of command as well. This may mean inviting someone to a meeting even when he or she has no obvious reason to be there; sending a copy of a memo to another manager as a courtesy; or asking a subordinate for advice even when you will make the final decision on your own.

Example: You report directly to a vice-president, who in turn reports to the president. Last week, the president approached you directly and asked for a report, to be delivered in one week. Your first step should be to advise your immediate supervisor of the assignment.

4. *Communicate with everyone who is affected by your decisions.* A common mistake made by managers is to overlook the need to let other people know what's going on. This can occur even when your intentions are pure. Before making a final decision about anything, take a moment to ask, "Who will be affected?" and spread the word accordingly.

Example: Your division's manager has given you the job of suggesting a reorganized floor plan for your department and two others on the same floor. Before proceeding, you meet with the two other managers, explain your assignment to them, and offer to let them review your proposed plan before you submit it.

5. *Think before you speak, then decide whether the timing is right.* Formulating a strong position is the first step toward protecting yourself.

When you do speak out, you will know that your position is sound. However, you also need to ensure that the timing is right. It is not always the message or how it's delivered that breaks the rules of etiquette; it may be the time and place.

Example: You will attend a staff meeting tomorrow at which you will have to explain why a project you are leading has fallen behind schedule. Today, you are not sure why it's behind schedule. Your priority is to gather the facts behind the delay and interpret them.

6. *Be aware that there are at least three agendas in every meeting.* Every meeting you attend—no matter how many others are present—involves at least three agendas. First is the written or stated agenda. As a matter of etiquette, everyone in the meeting should try to stay with that agenda, avoid letting discussions wander to other topics, and complete each segment on time. Second is your agenda. You want to achieve certain things in the meeting—that's one reason you attend. Be aware that what you want might conflict with the written agenda. Third is the agenda others bring to the meeting. You may have sound reasons for wanting to voice your opinion and gain a favorable decision. However, if the other attendees' agendas conflict with what you want, you may meet unexpected resistance.

Example: During a budget review meeting, one manager raised the question of increasing his staff during the next six months. This proposal came at the end of an extended discussion on the topic of salary budget overruns. The agenda of the meeting was historical review, not future change. The other attendees were concerned about *their* departmental budgets. The manager was not aware of agendas beyond his own; it consequently, was not the right time to bring up the idea.

CONFRONTATIONS

The etiquette of confrontations involves courtesy, apology at the appropriate time, and fair fighting. You achieve a great deal by defusing someone else's anger and by respecting that anger even when it is misplaced. If you allow yourself to be drawn into a negative confrontation—one focusing on personal accusations rather than issues—nothing positive can come from the experience. However, no matter how carefully or diplomatically you choose your statements or the time you make them, you will eventually find yourself in a face-to-face confrontation. In this situation, there are rules of behavior you need to follow.

1. Get your facts. If you are going to confront an issue with another employee, first make certain that you have all of your facts, and that you are right.
2. If you have made a mistake, apologize at once and try to defuse the other person's anger. Avoid having to defend a weak position. End the debate by accepting blame.
3. Learn to know when to apologize even when you are completely in the right but still want to apologize. It may come down to a question of being the more mature of two people in a confrontation.
4. Always stick to the issues. Confront problems, not people. In a family situation, this is called fair fighting. Constructive arguments are confined to the problems; destructive ones become personal. If you remember this distinction in a corporate argument, you will survive confrontations and achieve something positive from them.

These rules should be modified somewhat when confrontations take place across the lines of rank. For example, the vice-president might confront a manager, or an employee in your department might confront you. In these situations, it may be more difficult for the higher-ranked individual in the discussion to be the first to apologize. If one of the two recognizes that his or her behavior was inappropriate, however, an apology is still called for. Often, the lower-ranked person offers an apology—not always because he is in the wrong, but because of the difference in rank.

Example: During discussions with an employee in your department, you question the way a routine was performed. The employee explains that the usual procedure was not followed; her reasoning is sound. The employee apologizes, even though she had good reasons for taking exception to the usual methods.

In this case, the proper response is to help the employee to understand why an apology is not necessary. It is both courteous and appropriate to not let an employee give in to your rank, especially when no mistake was made.

Some sensible rules to follow regarding confrontations are summarized in Figure 1-2. These rules vary depending on your work environment and the relationships between people in the company. Some organizations survive with a high level of direct competition between departments and individuals, while others are more relaxed. (Much of the conflict in such companies, however, may exist in covert form.) You also need to be aware that the internal environment is constantly changing. A friendly, personal company may experience substantial change in a relatively short period of time if it experiences rapid growth; what is today a relaxed and cooperative environment can evolve into a more competitive one by next year.

Figure 1-2. Rules of confrontation.

1. Get your facts.

2. Apologize if you are wrong.

3. In some cases, apologize even when you're right.

4. Respect subordinates in a confrontation.

5. Always confront issues and not people.

FRIENDSHIPS AT WORK

One of the most distinct lines in most companies is the line between business and personal relationships. This line applies especially to the relationships between managers and their subordinates. This is not to say that it is impossible to develop close and lasting personal friendships through work; many people make their primary social contacts on the job. However, differences in rank do limit the possibility for true friendships; if you enter into a personal relationship with a subordinate, you may encounter supervisory problems on the job.

Example: A supervisor became close friends with one of the employees in his department. They went fishing together, invited each other to dinner, socialized regularly for several months. One day, under pressure of deadline, the supervisor told the employee to take care of a project. They argued, and an angry confrontation ensued. The supervisor realized, too late, that the personal relationship away from the job was interfering with his ability to supervise his staff properly.

In this situation, the disputants had different points of view. The employee probably believed the supervisor was treating him unfairly; the supervisor thought the employee was taking advantage of their friendship. Neither was completely right or wrong. The point is that the personal friendship clearly made the business relationship more difficult.

If you do begin a friendship with someone who reports to you (or to whom you report), remember this rule:

Keep a clear distance between the personal relationship and the business relationship.

You may be able to enjoy a close personal friendship with a subordinate or a superior without any consequences at work, provided that you both understand that the two relationships are separate and operate under different assumptions.

Even when the two employees involved are peers in terms of rank and title, an outside-the-office friendship can get in the way of a good business relationship. Again, this rule must be observed: The two forms of relationship do not operate in the same way and cannot be allowed to interfere with each other.

> **Example:** Two managers became close friends. However, when a conflict arose between their two departments, the friendship was affected, as well as the working relationship. They resolved the work problem and then agreed to certain rules. First, they would not discuss work when together away from the office; second, they would not carry disputes from one arena to the other; third, neither one would assume that the personal friendship would affect their behavior to one other in the company setting.

The problems of relationships away from the office are not limited to friendships. For example, what are the rules of etiquette when you get your job through a relative? One unspoken rule might be that such arrangements are not to be discussed openly. And if you are the person hired under those circumstances, another unspoken rule probably applies:

> When you've gotten your job through a relative, you have to try twice as hard as everyone else just to prove that you're worthy of the it.

People will assume, at least at first, that you wouldn't have been hired were it not for the influence Uncle Ted brought to bear.

MALE/FEMALE RELATIONSHIPS

Working with other people every day inevitably leads to attraction on many levels. It is inevitable that men and women will become friends. Remember, though, that if that relationship leads the friends to spend time together away from the office, everyone else will assume it's more than just a friendship.

Example: A married man and a married woman worked together in the same department and became good friends. The relationship was completely platonic; they even socialized with both spouses. However, because the two had lunch together frequently, a rumor began that they were involved romantically.

Even though this situation involves only idle gossip, it could affect both careers. Once a rumor begins, it's just about impossible to defuse it. In fact, if the people involved were to try, they would only make matters worse. The attempt to clear the air would not make the rumor go away; chances are that it would only lend veracity to it in the minds of others.

Another potential problem arises when one member of the corporate family is romantically interested in another, but the interest is not returned. An absolute rule should apply in this case:

<u>Unless the romantic feelings are mutual, the attempt to</u> <u>pursue the other person should be dropped without any</u> <u>second thoughts.</u>

This rule is easy to state but difficult to enforce, if only because an offending employee has not followed the rules of good behavior in the first place.

A difficult conflict arises when advances are made by one employee to another. Sexual harassment, especially when imposed by someone with power and influence on an employee with relatively little power, is exploitation. For the company, it raises questions of moral as well as legal jeopardy, since an employee who is being harassed may file suit against a manager or executive and against the company.

In some situations, the line between familiarity and sexual harassment is a thin one. To some people, being called "honey" is business as usual; to others, it is grounds for a lawsuit. When sexual harassment becomes a problem, unspoken rules should be put aside; more direct confrontation is necessary.

An employee who is being harassed by someone else has every right to ask that the advances stop. If that does not work, she (or he) should document all incidents and report them to her immediate supervisor. If the supervisor is perpetrating the harassment, it is appropriate to go over his (or her) head—to his supervisor, to the appropriate employee relations executive, or to the company attorney. This is one instance where the chain of command should be violated.

The employee who is being subjected to sexual harassment often believes—sometimes correctly—that her career will be in jeopardy if she reports the incidents. She may hope the harassment will stop on its own accord if she does nothing to encourage the offending person. This does not always work. She may need to take action, including requesting protection from the individual, accepting a transfer to another department, asking that the other person be transferred or even terminated, or asking for written assurances that the problem will not affect the status of her career. All of this is more easily said than done.

If your company's management is aware of the sexual harassment problem, it should be motivated to do whatever is needed to stop it, even if the offender must be terminated, if for no other reason than the severity of the legal consequences of taking no action.

Obviously, both men and women may be victims of sexual harassment. But what if the advance is made by someone of the same sex? In making a complaint, the employee risks exposing someone who may want to protect his or her sexual preference. A case of homosexual harrassment raises a more difficult problem for everyone than the more traditional heterosexual situation. In some cases, even making the accusation can expose the complainant to legal problems unless there is clear evidence to support the charge.

The rules of conduct in these uncomfortable situations are obvious. However, remember that the offending person is not following the rules and may be less sensitive to an appeal to reason or to the improper nature of his or her advance. He or she may respond only to a threat of further action.

These are highly personal issues that must be confronted are dealt with individually. As a potential victim, you have the right to assume the company will be on your side. However, if you find that the company is reluctant to take action, carefully document what happens, avoid giving the other person opportunities, and get yourself an attorney.

Of a less personal nature are politically motivated actions. These are not personal; the political motive involves the desire for power and influence, not the wish to resolve a problem with another person. Corporate politicking is the topic of the next chapter.

WORK PROJECT

1. What are the three popular myths about custom and the unspoken rules? What are the realities?
2. Name three of the six guidelines for defining company loyalty.
3. List three rules for dealing with confrontations.

2

Politics: Avoiding the Knife in Your Back

Always behave like a duck—keep calm and unruffled on the surface but paddle like the devil underneath.

—Jacob Braude

"I think the political problems in this company are finally getting to the boss," one employee whispered to another.

"Don't exaggerate," the other one replied. *"I mean, how bad can it be?"*

The first one pointed to the corner. *"Take a look for yourself. What do you see piled up around his office?"*

"Sandbags?"

Your company is a healthy, progressive, well-led organization, people-oriented and on the move. Top management is in touch, constantly striving to improve relationships with its employees; creative, bold, ambitious people are nurtured and encouraged. At least, that's what you were told when you were hired and that's what it says in the annual report.

The truth might be very different. Behind the facade of enlightened management, scenes of political intrigue may be played out daily, sometimes in a subtle and unspoken manner, other times in overt confrontations between managers or executives. Real motives reveal themselves in actions, not lip service. And the truly creative people may be punished, rather than rewarded.

The amount of political conflict varies from organization to organization, but its existence is universal. A relatively benign political climate may be disrupted by the addition of one difficult person at the executive or middle management level, or corporate politicking may be a nagging, constant, and ubiquitous reality. In any event, political conniving cannot be ignored; it is a problem that has to be confronted and overcome.

Your challenge is to identify the political activities in your company, become aware of their dangers, and decide how to act within the structure that exists. If you do not go through this process, you may find that it is not performance alone that determines how well your career progresses.

The truth is, of course, that performance should be the major criterion for success; in reality, success requires a keen awareness of the political realities that surround you. Only by striking a balance between performance and politics will you succeed.

CAUSES OF POLITICS WITHIN COMPANIES

There are many theories that claim to explain why a company becomes politically saturated and why the people within that company become players in the political game. No one cause can be easily identified; a combination of events and conditions is probably necessary to create the atmosphere for corporate infighting.

Most of us, hearing the word *politics,* immediately think of the negatives—power struggles, ambitious people doing one another in, and covert actions meant to make others look bad in the eyes of management. However, if you remember the rules of behavior, you will be able to identify a positive side to the political climate in your company and learn to use it to your advantage to improve, rather than worsen, internal relationships.

The causes of politics, summarized in Figure 2-1, include:

1. *Human nature.* Rivalry seems to be a natural state of affairs. Whenever a number of people are thrown together in an office or

Figure 2-1. Causes of politics.

```
1. Human nature.

2. Communication from the
   top.

3. Financial pressure.

4. Changes at the top.

5. Individual disruption.
```

anywhere else, conflict is sure to arise. It matters little if communication is very clear and everyone makes an effort to create an enlightened working environment; people will still find themselves at odds with others.

The solution: Accept the reality that people will not always act in the most positive way. Work around the negatives and emphasize a positive approach, both in the primary work of your department and the secondary work of understanding how to coexist with others. In seeking solutions to political situations, assume that the perpetrators of even the most devious acts want to have a sense of worth and would prefer to avoid conflict rather than create it.

2. *Communication from the top.* Much has been written about the need for communication from top management. However, maintaining open lines of communication is more difficult in practice than in theory. As soon as management stops keeping its staff informed and involved, a vacuum is created; this vacuum will be filled by someone seeking power. That's when politics infiltrates the layers of middle management and when people begin to think they must become political animals just to survive.

The solution: When top management fails in its primary purpose—to hold the company together and advance it toward its goals—plan to fill the resulting communications gap through helpful and creative leadership. If you allow the vacuum to be filled by ambition and infighting, the result will be negative. However, you and other managers can see to it that a different type of politics emerges—politics that helps rather than hurts the situation. It may become necessary to fill the void left by top management with a strong middle management version of leadership. Unfortunately, such efforts can lead to a segmentation in middle management layers in which one group sticks together and avoids the negative aspects of daily corporate life, trying to get along in harmony, while another group continues in its political ways. This segmentation may be unavoidable, but at least it protects a portion of the corporate family.

3. *Financial pressure.* Even when top management makes every effort to communicate with staff, circumstances may make it difficult to maintain this attitude. If the company is experiencing financial problems (loss of market share, lower-than-expected profits, cash flow problems, cancellation of a line of credit), top management's first impulse is often to circle the wagons and close down the lines of communication. This disrupts its healthy relationship with staff.

The solution: Make top management aware of the problem; appeal to reason; and encourage disclosure, even of bad news. Try to keep a focus on where the conflict belongs: between your organization and its competitors in the market, not inside the company. Staff wants to know what is going on; if they are not told, they will assume the worst from rumor and gossip. The only alternative to the rumor mill is to make sure the lines of communication stay open.

4. *Changes at the top.* Middle management and line employees become insecure when new top managers enter the scene. For example, assume a company hires a new president, who announces that sweeping changes will be made. The first tendency among employees—being unsure what these changes will mean—is to become nervous and defensive.

The solution: Set an example for subordinates by accepting change as inevitable. Give the new executive the benefit of the doubt. Also approach the new leader and offer yourself as a helpful resource during the transition. Look for positive methods for implementing the leader's worthwhile policies. Also, seek ways to deflect negative tendencies or politics. Don't add to your employees' insecurity by fueling their doubts; instead, look for a constructive way to take part in change.

A similar problem often occurs after a company is merged with or acquired by another. The new owner invariably sends the same message to employees: We don't intend to change the way you do things or to disrupt your routines. But inevitably, disruption does take place, often in a very big way. Over time, not only is the company's leadership replaced; the entire corporate philosophy may be revised as well, along with goals, standards, and methods of approaching the market. Underneath it all, the old politics will be replaced by new politics.

5. *Individual disruption*. It isn't just change at the top that triggers political action in the company. Anyone can start a series of events that affects everyone else. A single manager, motivated by ambition and willing to proceed ruthlessly, can bring out hostile reactions in others and disrupt an otherwise harmonious corporate style; staff, believing that others will behave in the same way, may act on the old idea that the best defense is a good offense.

The solution: Anyone who is motivated in solely by his or her own interests will probably not respond to reason, at least not right away. You may confront the problem in two ways. First, do not allow employees in your area of responsibility to be drawn into the political fight, under any circumstances. Second, verbalize the problem with the manager involved. Point out how his or her actions affect others. By doing this, you define, you draw a line for the other person, and you prevent allowing political motivations to run unchecked.

POWER STRUGGLES

The struggle for power and influence takes many forms in corporate life, including:

- Instigating individual rivalry
- Fomenting departmental or divisional rivalry

- Maintaining a high profile in meetings
- Competing for work and increased budgets

Dealing with each of these situations demands a different approach, since the situations develop from different causes. The solutions require application of a particular series of rules of etiquette.

1. *Instigating individual rivalry.* There is a human tendency to think of individual conflicts as battles of personalities. While such conflicts certainly may feel personal, you may need to detach yourself in order to deal with them.

Example: A newly-appointed manager of another department has adopted a very aggressive stance toward you. Your department works closely with the other department, and you realize that relationships will be strained unless you resolve the problem. However, when you try to communicate directly with the other manager, all you get is hostility.

Possible solutions: First, assume that the other manager is acting defensively and is expressing that feeling in an aggressive manner. Try to defuse the situation by making the relationship more personal. Invite him or her to lunch. Avoid confrontations during the meal, instead talking generally, perhaps about personal topics rather than business problems. Second, make a conciliatory gesture. If the manager is facing a particular problem of which you are aware, offer to help, or add your support to a worthwhile idea the manager proposes during a meeting. Establish the idea that you're willing to be an ally and that you are not a threat to the other person.

Etiquette in a one-to-one rivalry requires that you do all you can to establish rapport and avoid being pulled into the political game. If you behave in the same aggressive way as your would-be competitor, you will only convince him or her of the need for the rivalry, you will be equally culpable for the difficulties, and you will worsen the problem. But a sincere, well-motivated response will ultimately elicit a sense of trust and cooperation.

2. *Fomenting departmental or divisional rivalry.* Rivalries between departments often grow out of something that happened in the past or develop simply because communication is very poor, even when the two departments' work areas are physically close. Be willing to make an extra effort to defuse the situation, even if that means suspending otherwise rigid rules of procedure. Allow the rules of etiquette to prevail.

> **Example:** You are the manager of an administrative department. Word comes to you that the manager of a marketing department on the same floor has warned his employees that your area is the "enemy camp." As a result, the employees at the west end of the floor will have nothing to do with those on the east end.
>
> Possible solutions: Meet the marketing manager and look for common ground, either work-related or personal. Ease into a discussion of the current situation, and look for ways to eliminate the mistrust. The more you communicate in this way, the more you ease tensions.

The etiquette of defusing departmental rivalries is to avoid furthering a sense of mistrust. The leaders of each department are responsible for this effort, and you should be willing to make the first gesture. You may discover that there are good reasons for the bad feeling and that the difficulty can be resolved simply. For example, an accounting department may have held up salespeoples' reimbursement checks for procedural reasons; it may be in both departments' best interests to make an exception to the rules and rush through the checks. That small gesture will go a long way toward improving relationships. In this respect, the rule of etiquette should be: Take a flexible stance. Suspend the rules of procedure to improve the relationship.

3. *Maintaining a high profile in meetings.* For many people, meetings offer an opportunity to demonstrate leadership potential, or at least to bring attention to themselves as executive material. They may speak out boldly, take a stand against a proposal, or offer unusual recommendations, all in an effort to draw attention to themselves. This kind of attention–getting behavior can lead to many problems, especially for those who do not perceive meetings as auditions for bigger and better jobs and who must contend with the manager who believes he or she is "on" during the meeting.

Example: You have a recommendation to offer at a weekly staff meeting. Before the meeting, you met with other managers, explained your idea to them, and lined up support for your idea. During the preliminary discussions, several managers offered suggestions to round out your idea. You go into the meeting in the belief that you have the support you need. However, when you make your recommendation, one of those managers surprises you by raising points about the idea, clearly expressing his disagreement. You wish these points would have been brought up when you met with the manager beforehand.

Possible solutions: You may speculate about the other manager's motives, but that does not solve the problem. Chances are this behavior will be repeated in the future. You need to accept the reality that the other manager is not following the rules of etiquette, which include the idea that if you express support for an idea at one point, you should be prepared to back it up at a later time and not change your mind on the basis of who is present. In the future, you will have to proceed cautiously and assume that the other manager simply cannot be trusted to deal honestly with you.

The rule of etiquette in this situation is: Maintain your professional stance, and don't confront the other manager. Accept his or her shortcomings, but remember them in the future and prepare accordingly. As John F. Kennedy put it, "Forgive your enemies, but never forget their names."

4. *Competing for priority of work and increased budgets.* Some people equate receiving approval of a larger budget or priority for their work with having influence and power. To a degree, they are right. Problems emerge when people begin to compete with one another to gain influence and power.

Example: During a budget review process, your department's budget was cut, but another department's was raised. You were aware that, during the review process, the other manager fought for a larger budget and got it; you, in comparison, were not as vocal. The temptation, of course, is to make more noise the next time.

Possible solutions: Do not allow yourself to become a player in the budget game. That only makes you part of the recurring budgetary problem that management faces every year. Instead, work to stay within your budget. If you do need an increase next year, first do your homework—be prepared to support your request for an increase by demonstrating that profitability in your department will exceed that for the prior period, even with a larger budget, or that increases are necessary in order to maintain an acceptable level of quality and service.

The rule of etiquette in this situation: Play the game according to profit-motivated rules and the realities of the numbers. Don't compete on a political level. Ignore the fact that others may gain temporary advantage of being more vocal, and concentrate instead on doing your job to the best of your ability.

CORPORATE STATUS SYMBOLS

It can be extremely difficult to place yourself above the rivalry and anxiety that characterize corporate politics. The nagging fear persists that if you do not take part in the game, you will be forgotten, becoming the invisible manager who gets the job done competently but without enough splash to ensure that the president remembers your name.

This is a reasonable concern. In reality, though, the leadership and success you demonstrate *will* come to the attention of an intelligent and well-informed management team if—and this is a very big "if"—*if* you work for a company that is led by such people. One reality to always keep in mind:

The more fairness and awareness top management exercises, the less need there is for middle-layer politics.

Political maneuvering is most pervasive in companies whose top management responds to negative politics—satisfying the requests of the loudest and most troublesome people, for example. From this maneuvering, several corporate status symbols may emerge, including:

- *Power offices.* It's widely accepted that corner offices have greater status than mid-block ones. And managers with more square feet in their offices are for some reason presumed to have more power and influence than peers with smaller rooms.

- *Staff power.* Another political "rule" is that managers who increase their staffs beyond the size of those of their peers have greater influence, even if only in budgetary terms. The motive here is to create a high level of bureaucracy, the self-supporting busywork that demands more labor and less in the way of results.

- *Budgets.* If your department's budget is increased while others are forced to cut back, people will assume that your influence is on the rise. Again, this can lead to problems in the bottom line; as expenses grow, profits fall, and department managers will ultimately be blamed for the decreased profit margin.

- *Meeting attendance.* Being invited to the right meetings can be a sign of prestige in the corporate family. Great significance may be attached to the seating arrangement—even when seating is assigned on a very arbitrary basis. The meeting culture can create a middle-management class whose effectiveness is so low that it no longer manages—simply because it spends too much time attending meetings and not enough time back in the department, where the real work takes place.

Many presumed status symbols develop without any conscious thought on the part of top management. Giving a particular manager a "status" office is more likely to mean that the space was available rather than that there was some covert plan to show favoritism. Top management is probably too preoccupied with urgent business to give any thought to how it can convey subtle messages of approval or disapproval. Still, a degree of paranoia does exist among corporate employees, who assume that every action contains a message.

The rule of etiquette to keep in mind concerning status symbols is: Don't place too much significance on the location or appearance of things. Put your emphasis and energy into leading people well, getting the job done with an eye to quality, and communicating well with everyone. The less time you spend on questions about the appearance of influence, the better you demonstrate a professional attitude.

THE INFLUENCE GAME

Just as corporate status symbols become significant in peoples' minds, perceptions of influence play a big part in corporate belief systems. A good general rule to follow is: Emphasize performance, not appearance.

This rule is easy to state but hard to follow. Anxious managers, concerned that others hold more influence than they, may be diverted from the idea that performance counts and find themselves seeking more influence—sometimes in ways that could harm their department as well as their reputations.

> **Example:** One manager became alarmed when she discovered that memos from the president were being sent to the manager of another department. Her question was, "Why am I left off the distribution list?" The implication, of course, was that the second manager somehow held greater influence and that the first was in some way diminished. The manager was tempted to ask that her name be added to the list but decided against this course of action. She simply assumed that there were sound reasons for including the other manager.

The manager in this situation had no way of knowing why or how the other name was on the list. In a bureaucratic environment, adding names to a distribution list is easier than removing them; chances are the other manager's name had come to the president's attention many months before and had been included on the list and never removed. Now the name is on there permanently; it doesn't mean anything of importance.

The key point to remember is that the appearance of influence is just that—appearance. In the minds of the people whose opinion really counts—yours and the leaders of the company—status symbols have no real significance.

The rule of etiquette in this case is: Don't react to the appearance of influence by going out of your way to match what someone else seems to have. That takes away from your professionalism and only adds to the irritations that plague the lives of your company's executives. Grant management the courtesy of *not* playing the influence game.

NEUTRALIZING POLITICS

When you face a volatile political environment, you can choose one of two possible approaches. One is to compete within the structure, assuming that you have to take part in order to survive. The other is to try to undo the harmful elements of the political situation.

You can take several steps to neutralize politics. These are summarized in Figure 2-2 and include:

1. *Communicate directly with others.* One of the attributes of a highly political situation is poor communication. Messages, if sent at all, go by

Figure 2-2. Guidelines: neutralizing politics.

1. Communicate directly with others.

2. Don't play the influence game.

3. Don't worry about what others think or do.

4. Provide a positive leadership role model.

5. Present ideas from a position of strength.

6. Discuss new ideas with those affected by them.

a highly covert system; interpreting them takes energy and time; and confrontations are misdirected, avoiding the real issues rather than resolving them.

You can help solve this common problem if you begin improving the line of communication. Refuse to take part in the underground message system. If you have a message for someone else, deliver it directly, rather than falling into the trap of telling everyone except the person who is involved. This is a basic rule of etiquette: Speak to the right people, and only to the right people. Do not send messages through the ineffective and harmful corporate grapevine.

2. *Don't play the influence game.* So many people start out with the best intentions but nonetheless find themselves deeply involved in the internal competition game. Influence takes on such a strong importance in people's minds that they lose sight of their personal and career objectives as they scramble to achieve some illusory level of power.

The rule of etiquette is simple: Don't play the game, and don't allow a situation to take you over. It's poor politics, it misdirects your career path, and it sets a poor example. Put the same energy into improving your company's competitive stance, ensuring quality, and setting goals for yourself and for your department. Performance is the arena in which you really gain influence in the company.

3. *Don't worry about what others think or do.* Too much energy goes into second guessing within the company. No matter how much power and influence someone else gains, he or she cannot really harm you, your career, or your department—unless you want to play by the same rules.

Follow the rule of etiquette: Place company loyalty before your desire for power and influence. If you concentrate on what is really important, you won't have the time to worry about anyone else.

4. *Provide a positive leadership role model.* As a manager of a department, be constantly aware that your employees are watching you. The example you set will not only affect their behavior; it will also lead employees to draw a conclusion about the type of leader and person that you are.

The rule of etiquette is: Recognize your responsibility as a leader. Be aware of the high profile you maintain, and do all you can to set a good example.

5. *Present ideas from a position of strength.* Don't make yourself vulnerable to any attack. Although you don't want to take part in the negative politics that may be going on around you, it's also important to protect your position. This is one of the positive approaches to politics: Whenever you speak out, whether to recommend a new idea, ask for a higher budget, or criticize the way things are being done, first be sure you have all of the facts.

The rule of etiquette is clear: If you plan to speak out, first do your homework. Avoid any situation in which your own words can be used against you. Never start a discussion without a battery of facts, and never put yourself in a position of weakness when you open your mouth to suggest change.

6. *Discuss new ideas with those affected by them.* If you plan to offer suggestions for change in a meeting, first think about how the change would affect other departments. You will avoid a lot of trouble and bad reaction by discussing your ideas first with everyone who will be affected by the decision.

In a very political environment, you may not want to share ideas with others, fearing they will steal them from you. However, this is an extremely rare occurrence. If you think about it, there are many simple steps you can take to avoid having good ideas taken by someone else. For example, when discussing your ideas with others, don't give them a copy of the whole report; explain only those details they need to have in order to discuss the idea intelligently. You should take precautions when they are justified; however, you should not take security measures to such an extreme that you violate the rules of appropriate communication.

The rule of etiquette: Be constantly aware of the impact your ideas will have on others. Pay those affected the courtesy of presenting your ideas to them before taking the proposals to top management. You may find flaws in the proposal, in which case the preliminary dialogue may lead to improvement, or you may find allies in unexpected places.

Contending with the political aspects of corporate life can be exhausting and distracting. However, if you follow the rules you set for positive action, political maneuvering can be managed and controlled. One method for maintaining the proper focus is to respect the leadership structure or chain of command in the company. This is the topic of the next chapter.

WORK PROJECT

1. Explain three of the causes of politics in companies, and suggest possible solutions to them.
2. Discuss the etiquette involved in dealing with power struggles that develop in four areas:
    a. Individual rivalry
    b. Departmental or divisional rivalry
    c. High profile in meetings
    d. Priority of work and budgets
3. Describe three of the guidelines for neutralizing politics in your company.

3

Chain of Command: Identifying the Pecking Order

Come not between the dragon and his wrath.

—William Shakespeare

The manager was giving the newly-hired employee an orientation on her first day. "We're very aware of the chain of command in this company," he cautioned.

"That won't be a problem," the employee answered. "I'll be sure to tell you exactly what I'm doing."

"That's not what I mean," the manager said. It's the president. To him, the chain of command isn't just a reporting concept. That's what we call the whip he carries around."

The chain of command has two components. When you went into your first job, you were led through the routines and closely supervised. As you advanced, you gained freedom to work, think, and create on your own, although, when a problem came up, a boss was there to help you solve it. That's one side of the chain of command: Groups of employees are supervised and helped, given guidelines and work goals, and allowed to gain experience in a narrow range of effort.

The other side of the chain of command—respect for order and organization—is equally necessary in the company. From the executive point of view, the trick of operating within the chain of command is to minimize day-to-day contact with subordinates without losing touch with what is really going on in the company. Managers are in much closer touch with entry- and lower-level employees, to whom the chain of command may seem mysterious, powerful, and even unnecessary. Their task, then, is to create an understanding of how the chain of command works, why it is essential to respect it, and how to operate within its structure. Part of understanding the chain of command is knowing the rules of etiquette that should be followed.

FIRST AND LAST NAMES

One of the first challenges to the newly hired employee is figuring out whether to use first or last names. The traditional (and often outdated) rule is to always use last names when speaking to someone of higher rank. However, that rule rarely applies in today's corporation. Any one of several possible rules, summarized in Figure 3-1, might apply in your company. The possibilities include:

1. *Use last names for executives.* It is safe to say that use of the familiar first name is the rule for employees of equal rank. Any manager-to-manager communication follows this guideline without exception. However, when you are speaking to an executive, use the last name instead. This rule may apply in your company; the safest approach is to find out the rules first, even if that means asking.

2. *Use last names until told otherwise.* This is probably the safest approach if you are uncertain. If an executive prefers to be called by first name, he or she will tell you.

3. *Use first names for the next reporting level.* The traditional approach is to initiate contact by addressing anyone who outranks you by the last name. This is often impractical, however. If you manage a small department and are on familiar terms with employees, you wouldn't expect a newly hired employee to address you formally. However, an executive

Figure 3-1. Possible rules: first and last names.

1. Use last names for executives.

2. Use last names until told otherwise.

3. Use first names for the next reporting level.

4. Use first names universally.

5. Base your decision on the way letters to you are signed.

6. Decide based on what others do.

7. Ask permission.

supervising your department might expect a greater degree of formality from the managers under his or her control.

4. *Use first names universally.* In smaller companies, it is likely that everyone uses first names. One guideline is the degree of access that you and other employees have to the president or CEO. If you speak with the leader every day, you will probably find it more comfortable to use first names. In larger organizations, where you rarely if ever see top-level executives, use of the more formal name is more likely to be the rule.

5. *Base your decision on the way letters to you are signed.* The signal for use of first names might come from the way written communications

are signed. If an executive writes a letter to you and signs it with his or her first name, you should feel free to use the familiar style from that point forward.

6. *Do what others do.* If other people of your rank use first names when speaking to executives, follow their cue.

7. *Ask permission.* When in doubt, raise the question. You have the right to ask whether it is acceptable and appropriate to use familiar style. This is a better course than assuming first names are acceptable; being told to *not* use someone's first name is a humbling experience.

You may find yourself in a situation in which you are uncertain about the rules but nonetheless must refer to someone else. In that case, use the full name.

> **Example:** A recently promoted manager attended her first staff meeting. She reported on guidelines passed down by the CEO for a project assignment. Not sure whether to refer to the CEO as John or as Mr. Smith, she chose the tactful compromise and said, "John Smith has instructed us to. . . ." In later references, she used the title: "The CEO wants this project to . . ."

In this case, the manager was not certain whether to refer to the CEO by first name; to do so might violate an unspoken rule. However, if everyone else used the first name, the more formal reference would have been equally inappropriate—showing other attendees that she did not understand the rules. To escape this awkward situation, just ask another manager to explain the unspoken rule.

A related problem arises when you are expected to write a letter to someone whose sex you're unsure of. For example, how do you address a letter to G. Brown? The solution: When in doubt, use *the full name* in your salutation. Your letter to G. Brown should be addressed: "Dear G. Brown:".

Similarly, some first names are shared equally by both genders or are so unusual that you can't tell whether the person is a man or a woman. Do the same thing in this case that you did for G. Brown. Address a letter to Lee Jones as: "Dear Lee Jones:".

CORPORATE FAMILY RULES

Sometimes the chain of command works very well, but only in one direction. In other words, subordinates are given very specific rules and restrictions; proposed changes, complaints, suggestions, or questions must go through the immediate supervisor. However, executives do not follow the same chain of command, placing middle management in a difficult position.

> **Example:** In one company, whenever the president wanted something, he went directly to the employee and gave instructions in person—always with the highest priority. Managers were constantly discovering that their priorities had been replaced by the president's.

Diplomacy and self-preservation may prevent you from confronting this problem in the same way you would if the problem were with a subordinate. You cannot simply tell the president to stop violating the chain of command. However, there are some rules of etiquette that might prevent or mitigate the problem:

1. *Ask that instructions to your subordinates be passed through your office.* Managers have the right and the duty to ask that their positions be respected. This must be done with great diplomacy, however. There is always the danger that such a message will be interpreted as a power statement or as a complaint. No one wants to appear to be overly territorial; emphasize the need for order rather than your rights.

2. *Have subordinates ask for respect for the chain of command.* When subordinates are given tasks by someone other than their immediate supervisor, it places them on the spot. It's unfair to give two conflicting high-priority assignments to one person. It's also unfair to expect anyone to report to two different supervisors. Help subordinates by suggesting that any assignments they receive from other managers or executives should be made through you. If another person tries to give a member of your staff a work assignment, the person may explain that he or she has a conflicting task and deadline and that the request places them in a difficult position.

3. *Suggest procedures to protect subordinates from chain of command violations.* A nonpersonal recommendation might help prevent the problem from reoccurring. You could suggest to the president, for example, that assignments and requests should flow *down* the chain of command by the same rule that dictates that reporting moves *up* the chain.

4. *Deliver the completed task yourself.* When someone else gives your subordinate an assignment, you probably will have to allow the person to complete the job. However, when it is done, you should deliver the finished assignment yourself. Allowing the employee to deliver the finished product endorses and confirms the violation of the chain of command rule, whereas your delivering the assignment gives you the opportunity to gently suggest an alternative procedure. For example, you might say, "We'll be glad to respond promptly again. However, if you'll come to me next time, I'll be able to allocate resources without having to delay other deadlines."

5. *Present constructive solutions rather than complaints.* You may, for example, confront the problem by identifying the solutions offered the executive by the chain of command. As a rule, the fewer subordinates executives have to contact directly, the better. Suggest delegating not only work but also assignments—not just out of respect for your position, but also to make the executive's job much easier.

You may try these steps and still have to tolerate a disorganized executive. In some cases, you may have no choice but to accept the situation as a reality; in a smaller company, where the president whose office is a few feet away from your subordinate's desk may ask for something without thinking about the chain of command. By the same flexible rule, an employee in a small company might take a problem or request directly to the president. In such a setting, these interactions are to be expected. Any attempt to impose an overly formal structure in a small company is inappropriate.

INFLUENCE CENTERS

Outside of the chain of command and off the organization chart, there exists in most organizations an invisible series of relationships. They may exist because of personal relationships between the official power center and an individual; respect for individuals of a certain age who have a long history with the company; or titles.

> **Example:** In one very small company, the president hired his mother to run the bookkeeping department. Even though everyone was on a first-name basis, employees were expected to refer to the president's mother as "Mrs." This created an awkward exception to the general rule, as well as the kinds of problems generally created by nepotism.

This situation is uncomfortable for everyone. It violates all of the rules of etiquette and common sense, but there is little that anyone can do to solve the problem. It's one of those situations that you must tolerate and work around.

> **Example:** Among the employees in a processing department was one elderly gentleman who had been on the payroll since the early days. He did not hold a leadership position. However, he was acknowledged as a mentor-in-residence to everyone and anyone. The respect he received derived from his intimate knowledge of the company and its founders. He was invited to meetings even though he contributed nothing directly, and he was asked for advice on a range of ideas.

Some forms of corporate influence grow not from power and title, but from respect. It does not matter whether the person has a high rank or is a clerk. By the same token, rank and title alone do not automatically bring respect for the holder.

> **Example:** An engineering firm was organized not by departments but by project centers. Employees used first names when speaking to or about each project manager, with one exception. One manager was referred to as "The Colonel," a rank he had achieved in the Army. However, when people spoke to him directly, they used his first name. This is an example of a tradition that grew by practice and not from any rule. It was a courtesy.

You may be inclined to use a formal title when the name is accompanied by a designation. For example, you might work with two vice-presidents. With one, you are on a first-name basis; with the other, you use the more formal approach, only because he has the title "doctor." Given time and enough contact, you can revert to the first name or ask permission to use it. However, designations inhibit many people from using first names.

It's not only individuals who affect the chain of command, positively or negatively. In some cases, a department may be a center of influence, with links in the chain of command that are stronger than those in other departments.

Example: Annual budgets for each department are prepared in the accounting department. The power and influence held by that department are apparent, most obviously during the year-end period when budget research is underway.

In this case, one department holds influence over other departments *and* with the executive branch, at least while budgets are being prepared. In one sense, budget approval must go through that department, so the chain of command is extended or abridged. The influence and power are vested inappropriately in the accounting department. It spells trouble.

RESPECTING THE CHAIN OF COMMAND

Influence and power grow of their own accord and not as part of the chain of command. This can lead to problems within organizations, especially during periods of rapid expansion. In the interest of making the internal operation more organized and efficient, the company may sabotage itself by building "layers of caution," a chain of command that grows on its own without an underlying need.

A key point to remember:

The chain of command works only to the degree that it makes sense. As soon as structure replaces substance, the whole command idea begins to erode.

A command structure will be respected if it exists for logical reasons. As expansion occurs, management might react by attempting to create a more highly organized internal chain of command. This can lead to a number of problems, including:

1. *Isolation between top management and everyone else.* No one ever sets out to create an ineffective bureaucracy. It often happens, though, because management wants to improve the way that things are done. As business operations become more complex, management's first response may be to add more reporting layers and people; placing barriers between management and the rank-and-file at a time when communication should be improved.

2. *Ever-growing levels of reporting that add work but produce nothing else.* Middle layers easily become bureaucratic and ineffective. If these layers are added too quickly or if they simply aren't needed, a class of employee develops that has only one task: to write memos to one another.

2. *Constant growth in the number of employees and reporting levels.* Chains of command tend to grow. As a result, in times of expansion, staff expenses increase on top of the costs of ever-larger facilities and other related items. When the expansion stops or when operations must retreat, it proves much more difficult to reverse this trend.

4. *Loss of credibility with employees.* As a result of proliferating levels of management, the employees lose faith in the chain of command. They might be forced to operate within it, but its effectiveness is eroded.

These problems often do not have immediate solutions. If you find yourself in a situation where the chain of command is not working, the rule to follow is: Make the chain of command work within your department. Overall, the problems may be far beyond your control; however, you can still take steps to ensure that your own area of responsibility functions under logical rules.

How can you tell whether the reporting structure of your company is healthy? To determine how to proceed and what rules to establish and follow, ask yourself these questions:

1. *How effective is the reporting structure?* Are appropriate decisions made and actions taken when problems are revealed? Or is the process deferred in endless committees and task force meetings? The reporting

structure in your company can best be judged by the degree of freedom it allows. If the reporting structure contains too many layers of caution, action will be stifled. However, even a highly complex chain of command can act and react if it is well organized.

The rule of etiquette: Recommend guidelines for identifying problems and their solutions, for assigning actions, and for following up.

2. *How formal is the chain of command?* Does the power and influence structure exist on paper only? Or does your company place a lot of stock in titles, rank, rights of power, and procedures? In a very casual environment, it is much easier to take action and achieve results. In a highly formal one, protocol often must be respected, even when doing so means missing opportunities or failing to improve profits or take logical action.

The rule of etiquette: Recognize the style of leadership in your company. In a very informal culture, you will be relatively free to offer suggestions that lead to action. In a more formalized culture, you will need to work within the dictated structure. That means you need to think through a strategy before speaking out.

3. *Does it work in both directions?* In some companies, the chain of command must be strictly followed when reporting upward; however, from the top, it simply doesn't apply. Executives may demand response from anyone, and those in the middle are powerless to organize, control, or plan. This leads to chaos and loss of respect on all sides. In a better leadership environment, executives understand the need for structure and follow the rules.

The rule of etiquette: If you see room for improvement, make suggestions. But proceed carefully and offer your ideas with maximum diplomacy.

4. *Does the structure grow in times of business expansion?* When operations grows, the internal layers follow suit. However, if that growth is in layers of executives and managers rather than in essential support staff and departments, the company is in trouble; it's likely that, when expansion stops or reverses, it will be very difficult to reduce layers of caution.

The rule of etiquette: As you see staff size growing in times of expansion, offer suggestions to place limits on overhead. Emphasize the goal that expansion should be carried to the bottom line rather than being entirely absorbed by higher expenses. Confront the problem of expansion in overhead.

5. *Are executive layers growing more rapidly than rank-and-file?* In an attempt to improve a bad situation, top management may believe that it needs to hire more executives. Once the top ranks begin growing at a faster rate than the rank-and-file, the company is in deep trouble. In this situation, there is little that you can do to solve the problem except to hope that top management will realize its mistake before the entire operation is ruined.

The rule of etiquette: Share your observations with top management, going through the chain of command. Use the numbers to prove your point, rather than simply describing the problem. Propose solutions if you expect a positive response. Management looks to you for ideas; if you offer them in an appropriate manner, you are more likely to make your point.

BREAKING THE CHAIN

In some cases, even when the chain of command works well and is effective, you may be forced to violate the rule and go above someone's head. In these instances, there are two special rules to keep in mind.

First, document your actions. If a situation is serious enough to justify violating the chain of command, you need to carefully write down why you are taking that step.

Example: A female employee reports to a man who has been sexually harassing her. She asked him to stop, but to no avail. She has made notes on each instance, including the date and what was said.

Second, tell your boss you are going over his or her head. Also tell the person to whom you do report your concern that you are breaking the chain of command.

Example: The employee who is a victim of sexual harassment has not gotten the appropriate response from her boss. She informs him that, if he does not stop, she will go to his boss.

When she does take that step, she informs the executive that she is there without permission.

In this case, the employee had no choice but to violate the chain of command; the supervisor was the source of the problem. This dilemma may arise in a number of ways; an employee may discover that the boss is stealing money from the company or breaking the law in other ways. Obviously, confronting the offender in these situations might make the offense stop, but it is not the appropriate answer, as it does not remedy the problem.

It's possible that you might accidentally violate the chain of command. If that happens, your next action should be to defuse the situation as directly and as quickly as possible.

Example: You attend a meeting with your boss and are asked for an opinion concerning a problem. You offer your ideas and, as soon as you speak, see that your boss is upset and surprised. Then you realize that you did not share your thoughts with your boss ahead of time, making it look as though you are bypassing his authority.

If you find yourself in this situation, follow these rules of etiquette:

1. As soon as you have the chance, speak to your boss. Tell him you realized *after* you spoke that you had made a mistake. Explain that it was not intentional and that you will be more careful in the future.

2. If the same situation comes up again, respond by saying that you have some thoughts, but you want to discuss them with your supervisor before airing them in front of the committee. Also prepare for meetings by first meeting with your supervisor. If you have ideas, discuss them. Ask permission to voice them at the meeting, and do so only if given the go-ahead.

3. If a subordinate speaks out without first checking with you, take the person aside afterwards and explain why that creates a problem for you. Offer guidelines for the future—that before presenting ideas, the employee should discuss them with you. Encourage development of good ideas, but only within the existing chain of command.

Middle managers are constantly faced with the delicate task of balancing the chain of command. With both subordinates and supervisors to be concerned about, it is not an easy job. The rules of etiquette help clarify what is appropriate and what is not. Adding to the problem is the fact that the organization chart is only one reflection of the reporting structure. The influence centers in your company may be vastly different than the boxes and arrows everyone sees. This reality makes the rules of etiquette even more essential; they may be the only real guidance you can trust.

WORK PROJECT

1. Explain three possible rules to use when deciding whether to address others by first or by last name.
2. What are three rules of etiquette to follow when executives violate the chain of command?
3. List three of the five questions to ask to determine whether your company's reporting structure is healthy.

4

Let's Do Lunch: Digesting the Business Meal

A really busy person never knows how much he weighs.

—Edgar Watson Howe

The CEO met with several managers for breakfast at a local restaurant. "This salt shaker is our primary customer," he said, placing it at center table. "Let's think of new ways to get our product to him."

He continued explaining his ideas until, a few minutes later, their orders arrived. One manager whispered to another, "Please pass the primary customer."

You have only recently mastered the rules of behavior in your company, overcome your doubts about the unwritten code, and become completely at ease. Then the big day comes: You are invited to lunch with the company president.

This situation raises a new set of doubts and questions about the rules of etiquette. How much of the lunch will be a meal, and how much will be a test? What topics will be discussed? What subjects should you

46

avoid? Should you pay or even offer to pay? Should you order wine or just a soft drink? What if you spill your soup?

Until you understand the rules that apply during business meals, you may find these occasions even more intimidating than other meetings. Even after you've attended a number of business meals, you may still be less than comfortable.

INVITATIONS

As a general rule, the person who invites someone else to a business meal should pay. There are exceptions to this rule, however.

Example: An employee asks a manager for lunch to discuss a work-related issue. The manager in this situation should pick up the tab, unless the employee insists.

Example: A customer asks a salesperson to join him for dinner, and the topic of discussion is strictly business. The salesperson is justified in incurring the meal as a business expense.

Example: You invite another manager to a casual lunch for strictly social reasons. He brings his wife along. In this case, the other manager should offer to pay the bill, since he brought a guest.

Example: Two managers agree to have lunch together. Even though one advanced the idea, it is agreed in advance that they will split the bill.

When in doubt, you may offer to pay for a meal, even if you are invited. The question will often be settled in one of two ways: the direction in which the money or power flows or the relationship and position of each person (manager-employee, salesperson-customer, or vendor-employee, for example). Generally speaking, the higher-ranking individual pays for the meal, and the person representing the company picks up the tab when meeting with a customer. By the same generalization, a vendor pays for lunch with a purchasing agent.

The rules concerning invitations vary with the circumstances. In most cases, however, the rules listed below and summarized in Figure 4-1 apply.

1. *Reply promptly to the invitation.* Always give your answer as soon as possible after the invitation is made, whether you receive it verbally or in writing. Even an invitation in the body of a letter deserves a specific and prompt response.

2. *Give reasons for negative replies.* If you decline the invitation, give the real reason. Propose a later time if you have a scheduling conflict, too great a workload, or other reasons. If you must cancel or postpone an appointment made previously, do so as soon as possible. Apologize, and be sure to keep the second appointment.

3. *Make sure you know where the meal will take place and what rules apply there.* If there are any doubts about the luncheon environment, ask.

Figure 4-1. Rules for business meal guests.

1. Reply promptly to the invitation.

2. Give reasons for negative replies.

3. Make sure you know where the meal will be held, and what rules apply there.

4. Decline inappropriate invitations directly.

5. Be aware of who is controlling the agenda.

For example, you may be invited to a restaurant with which you are not familiar. If you are not certain how to dress, ask what type of place it is and plan accordingly. If the food will be exotic and, perhaps, unenjoyable for you, diplomatically ask the other person if he or she would mind changing locations.

4. *Decline inappropriate invitations directly.* If you believe the meeting would not be appropriate, say so and give your reasons. For example, suppose a male executive asks a female line employee to join him for a late dinner. The employee believes such a meal wouldn't be proper and should say as much, offering instead to meet during business hours and in the office—if, in fact, there is a business reason.

5. *Be aware of who is controlling the agenda.* Recognize the fact that, in most cases, the individual who pays for lunch also determines the topic and the course of discussion. If you are a guest, avoid struggling with your host for control.

You do not want to find yourself off guard, in a meeting environment you are not prepared for, or being forced to choose from a menu contrary to your diet. For example, if you are a vegetarian, you should make it clear that lunch at a steak house could be a problem for you. You might also find yourself completely unprepared for a meal meeting's agenda. In this case, the best response is to admit you need time to research, think about the issues, or consult with others. Promise a response and impose a deadline on yourself.

Example: A manager was invited to dinner by the president of the company. No agenda was mentioned at the time the invitation was made. During the meal, the president asked the manager's opinion on a number of planning questions. The manager responded to the best of his ability, then concluded by saying, "I'd like to give these questions some thought and get back to you with more details. Can I send you a memo in two days?"

In this example, the manager participated in the dialogue but also promised to respond further. This is much better than having to scramble to keep up and perhaps making statements or promises you will regret later.

When you take the first step and invite someone else to a business meal, a different set of rules apply. The agenda becomes your responsibility. Observe these rules, which are also summarized in Figure 4–2:

1. *Invite others for business reasons.* Make certain there is a business reason for the lunch, unless it is strictly social, in which case you should say so. When you do have a business purpose, disclose it at the time of the invitation. This gives the other person time to prepare for it or at least give some thought to the topic.

2. *Stick to the stated agenda.* If you explain the business reason for a meal, stick to the agenda at least part of the time. A business meal often involves only a brief discussion of the agenda item, then moves into a more relaxed mode. This is appropriate; however, avoid catching a guest off guard by bringing up business issues you did not mention at the time the invitation was made.

3. *Do not impose the idea on others.* Avoid making an acceptance seem mandatory if you invite a subordinate. That can be intimidating and

Figure 4-2. Rules for business meal hosts.

1. Invite others for business reasons.

2. Stick to the stated agenda.

3. Do not impose the idea on others.

4. Ask for a response as soon as possible.

5. Be aware of appearances.

unfair. Someone who reports to you might be extremely uncomfortable seeing you away from the office for a variety of reasons but might also be afraid to assert that sense of uneasiness. It might be more appropriate to first meet in the office, then ease into a meal meeting later.

4. *Ask for a response as soon as possible.* If you do not receive a response within a reasonable period of time, ask again. As the one offering the invitation, you have the right to an answer.

5. *Be aware of appearances.* A male and female going to lunch together frequently may take on the appearance of an intimate relationship, regardless of the truth behind the relationship. Also avoid favoritism. You may have sound reasons for inviting one employee to lunch more often than another; however, as a manager, you may need to invite others just as often.

APPROPRIATE BUSINESS MEETINGS

If you have a personal relationship with someone else at work, the rules of etiquette don't really apply. You are friends and not just business acquaintances. However, if you join someone else for a business meal, you should be aware of what is and what is not appropriate.

Observe these guidelines:

1. Late-night and weekend meals are usually not appropriate for strictly business meetings. A legitimate business meal should be tied closely to normal working hours: before-work breakfasts, luncheons, or after-dinner cocktails are acceptable in most circumstances.

Example: A manager asks an employee to lunch several times over a course of weeks. Then he proposes a Saturday lunch. The employee declines, stating that weekends are for family; unless there is an urgent business necessity, she prefers to restrict business meals to weekdays only.

2. Lengthy meal meetings away from the office should be allowed only when business topics are discussed during most of the time. If the

meal is business-related but largely social, the total time away from the office should be limited to the normal lunch hour.

Example: An executive was in the habit of inviting managers to lunch periodically, thinking that it would be easier to talk away from the office. His original intention was to have informal discussions about work-related issues. However, the luncheons became three-hour meetings involving little in the way of business and too much wine. Managers began declining invitations, and the executive finally realized his error.

3. Breakfast meetings are appropriate only in limited cases. An executive may ask managers to attend a brief breakfast to discuss specific issues, but it is an unfair imposition to invite someone to a strictly social meeting before work.

Example: The president of a small company often called breakfast meetings for selected executives and managers. Without exception, these meetings involved the discussion of issues to be dealt with that day. The breakfasts were usually brief and were all business.

4. After-work meetings in many varieties are appropriate, even when they are more social than business-related. An after-work cocktail is acceptable in many circumstances; dinner is less common. If a key customer, vendor, or employee is visiting from out of town, a dinner invitation is a hospitable gesture; for people with whom you work every day, such meetings are not common practice. A lunch is more common, if only out of respect for other's right to have dinner at home with their families.

Example: A manager often invited employees in the department for after-work drinks, especially when a work-related problem had come up. Away from the office, it was often easier to talk. However, he never asked an employee to have dinner, being aware of the extreme difference between the two meetings.

THE COMMUNICATION MEAL

There may be several different reasons for planning a business meal, and the true motivation for inviting someone to such a meeting often remains unstated. In some cases, when a direct business reason is operating, the result is the "working meal." These all-business gatherings can be extremely productive, assuming that all attendees are willing and able to tackle agenda items and get through them, arrive at decisions and a course of action—and then return to the office and put them into effect.

Often, however, meals serve a more subtle purpose. They are opportunities to confront problems gradually in an atmosphere more relaxed than the office, to discuss topics you do not want others to hear, or to avoid constant interruptions.

> **Example:** Two managers had a series of confrontations over a course of several months. Their objectives often were at odds, and contact to date had been nonproductive. They tried several face-to-face meetings in the office to resolve the conflict, with no positive results. Then one of the managers invited the other to lunch. They did not discuss any business issues during the meal but had a very casual discussion. As a result of the informal meeting away from the office, tensions seemed to ease. The meal did not solve the problems, but it did make it easier for the managers to communicate in the office more effectively.

This type of business, meal may be the most worthwhile. Sometimes the very environment of the office, with its constant stress and pressure, prevents two people from achieving progress; away from the office, they seem like completely different people.

You might notice that business associates are more relaxed as soon as they leave the office. If you have a high-pressure job, you probably feel yourself relaxing as well. A drink after work, a brief lunch, or even a coffee break with someone else can go a long way toward easing tensions—especially when similar attempts in the office have not worked. These out-of-the-offices gatherings often take place spontaneously.

TOPICS OF DISCUSSION

If business meals involved only business, they would be relatively simple meetings. However, unlike interactions in the office, these meetings present both an opportunity and a danger. The opportunity comes from the fact that it is easier to talk; there are fewer distractions, and the atmosphere is usually more relaxed. The same conditions make the meal dangerous, because you may be inclined to say things you wouldn't normally say in a meeting. Be aware of what you say and how you say it. Remember these rules:

1. *Do not gossip or speak out of line.* It is easy to forget the standards for professional behavior when away from the office, even with a co-worker. Apply the same restrictions on yourself that you practice in the office. Don't repeat rumors, gossip about fellow employees, or fish for information during a meal.

It is sometimes healthy to let off steam by complaining about a condition at work, even if that involves mentioning names. If you must take part in such a discussion, first be sure you know the other person well enough to take the risk. Remember, however, that if you have a complaint about someone, it would be more productive and healthy to find a way to speak to the person directly, rather than gossiping about him or her.

Example: Two managers met after work for cocktails. Both had experienced problems with a vice-president, and his name came up. They spent some time complaining about the problem and agreeing with each other's point of view. However, they also realized that the discussion itself actually prevented communication, rather than helping it. It made it more difficult to devise a method for making peace with the vice-president, thus actually solving the problem. A more constructive approach would have been to voice the concern, then come up with an idea for approaching the vice-president and offering a compromise or a solution.

2. *Assume your statements will be repeated.* A simple method for preventing yourself from saying something you will later regret is this:

Always assume that the other person will repeat what you say. No matter how well you trust someone else, the temptation to repeat gossip or idle talk can be irrestible. Don't set yourself up.

Example: A manager met with an executive during lunch. The president's new marketing expansion plan came up, although no specific agenda for the luncheon had been set. The manager complained that he thought it was overly aggressive, costly, and premature. The following day, during a committee meeting, the president said to the manager, "I understand you have some doubts about the expansion plan." The manager realized at once that he'd said too much at lunch and that he should have expressed his concerns to the president directly.

3. *Avoid overly personal topics.* Remember that a business relationship is *not* always the same as a friendship. Unless you know someone you work with extremely well and on a very personal level, avoid very personal or controversial topics during a business meal. These include marital problems, addictions, health problems, personal religious beliefs, and anything else that is no one else's business. Even if the other person is receptive to your statements, they do not belong in a business meeting—either in the office or during a meal.

Don't let the relaxed atmosphere of a restaurant lull you into suspending cultural limitations that separate business and personal matters. Many people have spoken too much or too soon, only to see their indiscretions affect their professional reputations and relationships.

Example: While having a cocktail after work, a manager and one of the employees in his department discussed a variety of topics, mostly unrelated to work. During the conversation, the manager told the employee that he and his wife were going through a divorce. He noticed over the next few days that the employee was avoiding him. He realized—too late—that his bringing up an extremely personal problem had been out of line. It violated the unspoken rule of separation between business and personal relationships.

DECIDING WHAT TO ORDER

Should you order the eight-dollar rainbow trout, which you really don't want, or the forty-five–dollar steak and lobster? This question will come up in your mind whenever someone else will be picking up the tab. You don't want to order a meal you really don't want; you also do not want to take advantage or appear to be doing so. If this question does disturb you, choose a meal that falls in the medium range. If you select the least expensive item on the menu, your host may believe that you did so because you were uncomfortable; if you pick something you will enjoy that is not especially expensive, the question won't come up.

One point to keep in mind: When the other person invited you, assuming that he or she selected the restaurant, the range of prices was (or should have been) known. So if you are taken to a very expensive restaurant, you should not struggle with the question of price.

Also at a business meal, you should avoid foods that are awkward to eat. For example, you might want ribs or corn on the cob; resist the temptation and pick a meal that won't require the use of your fingers.

It may be inappropriate to order certain foods, even if they are on the menu. For example, you may end up in a very upscale restaurant with white tablecloths and candles on every table. Even if a cheeseburger is on the menu, you should probably order the filet mignon instead.

If you are a guest, never complain about the service or the food. If your meal is not properly prepared or is indigestible, or if your order is not correct, you should ask the waiter to correct the problem. However, don't insult your host by commenting any further. If you are the host, however, you have more latitude. You may be extremely embarrassed at having brought a business associate to a restaurant that is below standard. Some guidelines for hosts:

1. *Always make reservations in advance.* Plan your appointment well in advance. Call the restaurant and make reservations. Call again on the day of the scheduled meal and confirm the appointment so that you will not have to wait. If you don't make reservations, you may not be able to patronize the place you had in mind. Having then to go elsewhere will make a poor impression on your guest, suggesting poor planning and lack of concern.

2. *Take guests to restaurants where you have eaten before.* Hosting a business meal is not the time to indulge your curiosity about a restaurant you've never tried. Choose high-quality establishments where you have eaten before. If you know the owner or manager, make a point of staying in contact; make reservations directly with your contact; and say hello and goodbye to your contact as you arrive and leave. The personal touch and customer loyalty go a long way toward ensuring extraspecial service.

3. *Leave the appropriate tip.* If service was at or above par, leave a 15 percent tip. If paying by credit card, you may either add the tip to the total on the check or leave cash at the table. If service is poor, reduce the percentage of the tip accordingly. If you know the owner or manager personally, you may inform him or her of the problem, but take care of that later and not while you are with your guest.

4. *Apologize if the food or service is below par.* Even in establishments you know well, the food or service on one particular day may be below your expectations. If this occurs, explain to your guest that you patronize the restaurant regularly, and that this is not typical. Apologize for the problem.

5. *Select the right setting.* Most business lunches will take place in comfortable settings—not overly expensive or intimate, and not too cheap. You certainly would not want to call a business lunch at a fast food restaurant, and probably not at a top-of-the-line club where the wait is forty-five minutes, even with reservations. Select an unpretentious and medium-priced restaurant for most lunches. Choose a somewhat higher-priced location for dinners, especially when entertaining key customers, executives, or vendors.

For hosts as well as for guests, the question of whether or not to order alcohol is difficult. For example, you might find yourself invited by the president of the company. He may be completely opposed to drinking, or might feel very strongly that employees should not drink at lunch.

There is a very simple way to tell who is in charge at the business meal. When the waiter asks whether anyone would like a drink, there is usually an awkward pause. No one wants to speak out first; the one who does either is in the stronger position or does not fear the possible consequences of having a glass of wine.

Whether you are a host or a guest, remember these rules:

1. *Determine whether there is a company policy regarding drinking at lunch.* Some companies, through either a written policy or the unwritten standards set at the top, disapprove of or forbid employees to drink alcoholic beverages at lunch. If you are not sure about the rules, find out the answer before you go. It may be that no one will inform you if you break an unwritten law, so it's wise to know that law before you go to the meal.

2. *If you do have a drink, limit yourself to one.* You might be able to handle two or three glasses of wine during lunch. However, in a business situation, you should limit consumption to only one drink. Going beyond that level may make a negative impression on others at the table. Not only might it seem excessive; drinking might loosen your tongue more than is in your best interests.

3. *If in doubt, order a nonalcoholic beverage.* Take the safe route if you simply don't know. A soft drink, water, or coffee won't offend anyone or break any unwritten rules.

4. *If you will drive after the meal, do not order any alcoholic beverages.* As a good general rule, do not drink if you will be driving after the meal. This is not only a safety point; it also may affect your business associates' opinion of you.

5. *Don't have a drink if you don't want one.* You may sense pressure to have a drink even if you don't want one. If a business associate encourages you to drink, you can deal with the problem in several ways. You may say you don't drink, that you have to drive later, or that drinking disagrees with you. In any event, don't allow others to pressure you into having a drink you don't want.

UNINVITED GUESTS

If you are a guest at a business meal, you should never ask someone else to join you unless you first check with your host. Even then, it is not proper in many cases to even make the suggestion.

Example: You have been invited to lunch by an executive in your company. The main agenda topic will be an upcoming change in a product line that will affect your department. You believe that one of the employees in your department should attend, as her job will be most affected by the changes. However, resist the temptation to suggest bringing her along. It would be better to arrange a second meeting, if appropriate.

If you are the host of a business meal and your guest shows up with someone else—an employee, manager, or spouse, for example—do not comment at the time. However, you may discuss the situation later, mentioning that you had intended to discuss specific business issues and that the presence of an additional person prevented you from doing so.

An awkward situation arises when others invite themselves. How do you deal with this without offending the person or making a guest uncomfortable?

Example: You have invited an employee in your department to lunch away from the office to discuss a six-month evaluation. As you begin your meal, a fellow manager spots you and comes over to your table. "Why don't I join you?" he says.

The easy way out of this situation is to respond positively and simply abandon your agenda. By tolerating the intrusion, you at least avoid rejecting someone else. It might be considered good politics to take this course. However, it also means accepting an unfair intrusion. An alternative is to decline assertively, without hurting the other person's feelings. You may say, for example, "I'd be delighted, but the timing isn't good. We're having a meeting about a six-month evaluation. Can we get together for lunch tomorrow instead?" This is a gracious way out of the situation. Not only do you give an explanation, but you extend an invitation for lunch in the near future. You also avoid having to confront the uncomfortable fact that the other person tried to invite himself to your table.

The pressures and decisions you face in trying to deal with the unspoken rules surrounding business meals can make them unenjoyable. The solution is to prepare, set an agenda (as a host) or understand the agenda in advance (as a guest), and pay special attention to the social aspects of the meeting. If nothing else, living through the business meal will make you appreciate the relaxation of eating at home.

WORK PROJECT

1. Explain three of the rules for business meal guests, and explain how behavior is affected by those rules.
2. Discuss three of the rules for business meal hosts.
3. List three points concerning consumption of alcoholic beverages during a business meal.

5

Appointments: Making Eye Contact in the One-to-One

If we do not find anything pleasant, at least we shall find something new.

—Voltaire

Two managers agreed to meet for lunch at twelve noon. One was late, so they weren't seated until 12:20. The tardy manager declared, "I've decided not to make any more appointments for the rest of my career."

"That sounds pretty drastic," the other one replied. "What made you come to that decision?"

"As you know, I seem to have a problem showing up on time, and I've simply run out of excuses."

You have an appointment. It isn't enough to write it down in your date book and then simply show up. You also have to decide whether to be late (and, if so, by how many minutes) or to take the most drastic step of all and show up on time.

Virtually everyone agrees that promptness is a positive attribute. However, when it comes to business meetings, being a little bit late—in other words, keeping the other person waiting—often is viewed as a

61

statement of power and influence. The common courtesy of being on time is abandoned. The nonverbal statement made by the way appointments are kept is one of the complexities of the corporate culture. Some people are simply disorganized and cannot stay on schedule. Others may be expressing seniority or power by keeping you waiting. There is no simple way to know which of these two possibilities applies in each case, but there are logical rules of etiquette worth observing.

The etiquette of appointments also involves rules on preparation and follow-up. How you handle these critical aspects of your professional life will have a major impact on your success.

RULES OF PROMPTNESS

Corporate folklore dictates that keeping someone else waiting for a meeting is a nonverbal power statement. Being the one forced to wait, by the same rule, is often seen as an admission of being at a disadvantage. Too much can be made of this idea. However, even if the belief is held in your company, it is not necessary to alter your standards or your behavior. Even when being early, on time, or late does make a statement, you do not need to play the game.

The general assumption about promptness includes these ideas:

1. The person who keeps someone else waiting has either the advantage or more power. Thus, it is in your own benefit to show up late.

2. The person who shows up early for an appointment is at a disadvantage. Accordingly, being late is better than being early.

3. If you show up exactly on time, that tells the other person that you are overly precise or, perhaps, anxious. Promptness places you in a weak position.

None of these generalizations is necessarily true. The rules of common courtesy should be of greater importance in a business setting. These rules include:

1. Showing up early is better than showing up late. You may be kept waiting until the scheduled time; however, you're not giving up influence or power by demonstrating courtesy.

2. Being on time is extremely important. It conveys the message that you respect the other person's time. Being prompt is professional behavior.

3. Being late for an appointment may be unavoidable on occasion. When you are late, you should apologize.

The myths that have developed around promptness (or the lack of it) and the power/influence question affect behavior to the point that, in many companies, practically no one is on time for appointments.

Example: In one company, managers and executives were late so consistently that an agreed appointment time lost all meaning. It was not unusual for meetings to convene as much as thirty minutes later than the scheduled time.

The consequences of consistently being late for appointments include loss of productivity, delays in meetings and appointments later in the day, failure to meet each day's priority goals, and the creation of a sense of personal inefficiency. Even if you assume that, in fact, your being early or on time for an appointment gives the other person some kind of advantage over you, consider these points:

- Any intangible power–oriented advantage is more than offset by the advantage you gain by the courtesy statement you make by being on time.
- Showing up on time is professional, no matter what power and influence forces are at work.
- Those who pay attention to power and influence at the expense of good manners add to the problem.
- Promptness sets a positive example for your subordinates. If other people report to you, it's more important to be aware of their impression of you than it is to make a power statement to others.

APPOINTMENT GUIDELINES

Power and influence are very real issues in the corporate world. Seeking power is negative and destructive behavior, but being aware of the power-seeking behavior of others may be necessary for you to survive in the politically charged environment of the company. The competitive forces around you cannot be ignored; however, they can be put in perspective and controlled, respected, and understood so that you can live by the unspoken rules without having to compromise in your own behavior. You can do this if you develop a series of guidelines by which you will operate. These guidelines should not vary with the rank or position of the person with whom you have an appointment.

Example: One manager found herself using a different standard of behavior for different company employees, depending on rank. When meeting with the president, she was never late and never early. However, when meeting with a subordinate, she often delayed the meeting by five or ten minutes.

In this example, the manager fell into a common trap: altering behavior in response to rank. This is allowing the power and influence game to change you, rather than accepting but applying sensible rules of behavior. Awareness of rank can go against the logical rules of etiquette. You must be aware of rank, but courtesy should be the standard for your behavior. Some suggested guidelines, which are also summarized in Figure 5-1, are:

1. *Apply the same standards to everyone.* Once you alter your behavior on the basis of the rank of others in the company, you lose the awareness you need to be an effective, fair member of the corporate culture. Good rules apply to everyone. You cannot ignore rank, but you can set fair standards and then practice them.

Example: A manager kept a subordinate waiting for twenty minutes because he was in another meeting that ran longer than the scheduled time. He apologized and explained the reasons, adding that he would do his best to be on time for their next meeting.

Figure 5-1. Appointment guidelines.

1. Apply the same standards to everyone.

2. Adopt a customer service attitude, both externally and internally.

3. Be more aware of good manners than of power and influence.

4. Don't allow others to keep you waiting unreasonably.

5. Always apologize when you are late.

2. *Adopt a customer-service attitude, both externally and internally.* You may find yourself treating external customers exceptionally well and applying different standards for those in the company. If any other departments or divisions depend on you for information or work (and virtually all departments fit this description), recognize the importance of the internal customer.

Example: The manager of the accounting department met with the manager of marketing and sales at 1 P.M. every week. She was never late for this appointment, believing that the other department was an internal customer in the same way that someone outside the company was a customer to the marketing department. This attitude created an environment of mutual trust and respect.

3. *Be more aware of good manners than of power and influence.* Power and influence exist and serve a function. They affect our behavior and bring order to the company; without them, nothing could ever be accomplished. However, you need to separate your awareness of power and influence from the importance of consistently courteous and respectful behavior.

Example: A manager showed up on time for a meeting with the head of the finance committee. The meeting had been called to solve current budgeting problems. The manager was tempted to come five minutes late, being aware that the other person disagreed on some of the issues on the agenda. However, he ignored this hunch and made a better impression by demonstrating common courtesy. He gained more influence by showing respect for the other person's time than he would have been by making his own power statement.

4. *Don't allow others to keep you waiting unreasonably.* You deserve to have others respect your schedule, too. If you have an appointment, decide how long you should wait before leaving. For example, a ten-minute delay might not be unreasonable; a twenty-minute delay could be a different story. Leaving after waiting for a while should not be a power and influence issue; it is a statement concerning courtesy. The other person owes you an apology, but that won't necessarily come. You may have to reschedule the appointment yourself.

Example: A manager had an appointment with a vice-president for 3 P.M. By 3:30, the vice-president hadn't shown up, so the manager returned to her department. She was tempted to continue waiting, because of the executive's position; however, she had other important work to get done that afternoon and could not wait any longer.

5. *Always apologize when you are late.* Although it is not common in today's corporate culture, consider adopting the attitude that promptness

is extremely important to you. It may seem unimportant to many others; you may conclude that some people are not even aware of the importance of promptness. Set a rule for yourself that, except when it is unavoidable, you will never be late for an appointment. Gain reputation for promptness, and it will become a sign of professionalism. Others will understand the ethic and respect you.

> **Example:** One manager always left for appointments early enough to ensure her being on time. She was often a few minutes early but was late for only two appointments during the past year—once when another meeting ran late and she couldn't leave on time, and once when her car broke down on the freeway.

THE UNSCHEDULED APPOINTMENT

Another popular belief among managers and executives is that a powerful or influential person should not make appointments casually and should routinely delay meetings for several days, even if he or she has time available today. The myth states that an "important" person cannot see people at a moment's notice; they have far too many things to do to be that flexible.

With that myth in mind, it can be difficult or impossible to arrange a spontaneous meeting; the other person may not be willing to admit that his or her time is free enough to respond at the moment and may insist that the appointment be made for another day. As a consequence, you may not be able to act as freely as you would like. You may have to go along with the other person's need to appear powerful and accept the delay. It's not productive or efficient, but it might be a reality.

One unspoken rule of etiquette might be: Never ask for an unscheduled appointment. This is not a fair rule, but it may be practiced in your own corporate culture. You can get around this rule, however, when you have truly urgent behavior.

> **Example:** A manager needed to meet with the vice-president to ask for guidelines for a project she'd assigned. He visited the vice-president's office and asked for an appointment. "When do

you want to get together?" the vice-president asked. With that opening, the manager answered, "Right now would be best, if you have the time. I'm up against a deadline but can't proceed until after we've met."

In this example, the vice-president has the opportunity to take care of the problem at once, rather than putting it off. If her schedule permits, that might be better than having to contend with it later. The manager also stressed the importance of staying on schedule with the project in order to meet the final deadline—a compelling reason to hold an unscheduled appointment.

If the unscheduled meeting is urgent enough, you will be able to overcome the other person's desire to delay it. It's just a matter of appealing to reason. However, you also need to respect the other person's time constraints. You may have to accept a limit on the total time you will be able to spend when the appointment is spontaneous.

Example: You need to speak with the president urgently. An upcoming deadline cannot be met until an important decision has been made. You visit his office and explain that you need fifteen minutes. The president agrees but adds the provision that, at the end of the quarter hour, he has to leave for another meeting.

You may be forced to impose similar restrictions when someone else requests an immediate appointment—not for reasons of power and influence but because you have other commitments. Be sure to communicate these conditions specifically, explaining why they are necessary. However, avoid the temptation automatically to delay a meeting that is truly urgent or to place a time limit on an unscheduled meeting when it isn't necessary.

Even when an appointment is requested without a sense of urgency, make allowances in the name of convenience. If you have the time, you lose nothing by agreeing to meet with someone else. That does not imply that you aren't busy. It does demonstrate that you possess the flexibility and organization to meet with someone else without requiring advance notice.

If unscheduled meetings become the rule rather than the exception, gently encourage others to plan ahead a bit, even if by only one day.

While you want to remain as flexible as possible, unplanned appointments can interfere with your control over your time. There will be days when you simply won't be able to accommodate the other person. Make sure you explain why you cannot meet without notice; set an appointment for the earliest possible time.

> **Example:** Another manager has dropped by your office several times during the past month to discuss a project you're working on together. You would prefer scheduled appointments, since these meetings are beginning to interfere with recurring priorities in the department. At the end of the most recent meeting, you concluded by saying, "Let's schedule another appointment in a few days. That way, I'll be able to set the time aside."

In a case like this, you might have to refuse to see the other person, if only to enforce your request. Again, this is not a power and influence statement but is made necessary by your need to plan and control time.

In many companies, large and small, there is enough informality between departments and rank that unscheduled appointments do not pose a problem. In that case, the need for advance planning and appointments does not exist. However, as your company expands its markets and employee base and as the internal staff becomes more highly structured, formality may not be far behind; and you might need to accept the less desirable rules as a consequence of otherwise positive growth. When more employees are working in the company and when higher levels of responsibility are delegated, people tend to need and want more structure in their daily routine. Be aware of the rules as they stand today, but be on the lookout for signs of change in the environment and in the rules.

> **Example:** In one company, there was rarely a need for structured meetings. There were few people and they worked closely together. However, expansion has occurred during the last two years, and many more employees were hired. Now, there is a need for a more structured environment, and appointments are often necessary before meetings can take place. The expanded environment restricts everyone's ability to get together without notice.

PROPER PREPARATION

Whether you set an appointment with someone else or accept the commitment at another's request, be prepared for the agenda that will be discussed. Being late for your appointment may be poor manners; being unprepared is far worse. However, some meetings cannot be prepared for, because the agenda is not specific enough. The exact issue may not emerge until the meeting is underway.

> **Example:** An employee in your department has asked for a meeting to discuss his work. During the meeting, the employee tells you he is very unhappy with the assignments he has been given and asks you to switch assignments around. You explain that the request is not a simple one and that you will need time to think about a number of issues: whether it is fair or appropriate to make a change, how any reassignments would be made, and the reasons that the employee is not happy.

Every manager eventually faces difficult supervision problems that come up unexpectedly, making preparation for the meeting impossible. A possible solution: Promise to consider the request, investigate, and meet with the employee again in a few days. Schedule another appointment at the conclusion of the meeting.

Many types of meetings do require tangible preparation. In those cases, a rule of etiquette to remember is: Be ready for the meeting, without exception. If you cannot be ready for any reason, postpone the meeting with as much advance notice as possible.

> **Example:** The president assigned a project to you several weeks ago. He has made an appointment with you to review progress to date and has asked you to prepare a brief report. The day before the meeting, you realize you won't have the report completed in time. So you contact the president and ask for a one-day postponement.

If the meeting cannot be postponed, you may have to show up as prepared as possible—even if that means not having the work requested.

For example, the president in the example above might respond by saying the meeting cannot be delayed. Your choice: Either get the report completed that evening or show up with a partial report. Avoid going to the meeting with nothing to show. Worst of all is showing up unprepared without having first asked for the postponement you need.

KEEPING YOUR PROMISES

Every appointment contains an explicit series of promises: to attend the meeting and to arrive on time, to participate in the topics to be discussed and resolved, and to be as prepared as possible for the meeting itself. In addition, you may make a number of promises during the meeting, such as taking action on an agenda item, setting the time for a subsequent appointment, or preparing a report, memo, or other written response. Any follow-up promised by you or by others should be confirmed in writing. You can take care of this task, whether the promises were yours or someone else's. This is nothing less than good, sensible policy. It is also a point of etiquette. After the meeting, write a brief memo to verify and to remind the other person—and to provide a chance for the recipient to disagree if he or she did not understand the promises the same way you did. Even when you believe that communication was very clear, someone else may have come away from the meeting with different conclusions.

Example: You attended a meeting with another manager yesterday. As you understood it, the manager was going to prepare a brief report and send a copy to you. In a memo, you outline the conclusions reached. The other manager then telephones you and states, "I thought we agreed that *you* would prepare the report."

In this case, the other manager left the meeting with a conclusion that disagreed with yours and even contradicted it. This is *not* uncommon. The problem points out the need to verify and put in writing exactly what promises were made and by whom and what actions will be taken. This protects both sides, improves communication, and ensures that promised actions will be taken.

Writing a brief memo provides a chance to demonstrate another point of etiquette. It is a chance to express your thanks to the other person for attending the meeting and for working with you. You can state your thanks in the first sentence of the memo and follow with an explanation of the memo's purpose: "Thank you for meeting with me yesterday morning. This memo is to confirm the mutual conclusions we reached."

After this introduction, list the major topics and the results of discussions and agreements. Explain the actions you will take, as well as the follow-up actions the other person agreed to undertake. Then conclude by requesting that the recipient verify that the summary is an accurate description of what took place during the meeting. If the other person disagrees on any points, ask him or her to get in touch with you immediately so that the problem can be resolved.

FOLLOWING UP

A productive meeting concludes with agreement on some course of action, on who will assume responsibility for taking that action, or on what the next step (in solving a problem, finding information, or satisfying a requirement) should be. Thus, after your appointment, you should expect to have a task to perform—even if that task is to ensure that someone else follows through as promised. Under those circumstances, the rule of etiquette should be: Always follow through as you promise. Also be sure that, whatever the task, you complete it by the agreed-upon deadline.

If you have attended more than just a few meetings, you already know that the follow-up is the most critical part and that, all too often, nothing is accomplished by meetings. You can change those conditions, but only within the narrow restrictions of your corporate culture and its rules.

Example: A manager is upset that after a series of meetings, no action has been taken—even though assignments were given out to various people. The manager complains about this condition.

This is probably the least effective way to create change. In addition, it breaks an unspoken rule of etiquette at work in many companies: The complaint was made against an existing practice and in a negative manner.

A more positive approach is to create conditions in which positive results are not only possible, but more likely. Writing a follow-up verification memo is one way to have an effect on other people. If they don't respond to your memo, follow up with a phone call or visit. *Ask* for an answer. Make sure that others know what you expect as the result of your participation.

Another method is to provide an example. As a diligent and professional employee, you will do best by taking your responsibilities seriously. That means coming through on promises and meeting deadlines. Even if others do not apply the same standards to themselves, you can set an example for them as well as for your subordinates. This method does not break the unspoken rules of behavior; it *does* demonstrate that you take your job seriously, and that you know what's expected of you.

These ideas will be expanded and discussed further in the next chapter. As far as appointments are concerned, remember these points:

- Always respect the value of other people's time. Express that respect by showing up for appointments on time and prepared. Make this a personal standard for professional behavior.
- Forget about the power and influence issue involved with being early, on time, or late. Concentrate instead on professional behavior and courtesy. They will get you much farther than any appearance of power and influence.
- If you are late, apologize and explain. If someone else is late, give the person a reasonable amount of time and then go on to the next task—because of the need to manage your time, rather than as a power play.

- Allow unplanned appointments if you have time in your schedule. However, encourage other people to make appointments if they abuse the courtesy.

WORK PROJECT

1. List the three assumptions about promptness, and explain why they are often wrong.
2. Explain three rules of common courtesy concerning promptness.
3. What are three appointment guidelines worth remembering?

6

Meetings and Conventions: Coming Back Alive

There is no better place in the world the find out the shortcomings of each other than a conference.

—Will Rogers

"I'm a little worried about the boss," one employee whispered to another. "I think he's going to too many meetings."

The second employee replied, "He's having one right now in his office. I can hear his voice."

"Yes. But he's alone."

You've been invited to a meeting. But this isn't Christmas at Aunt Martha's house. There are no presents under the tree—just a big table and a lot of people dressed in gray, jotting notes on legal pads. And they want to know only one thing: Where did you spend all that money?

To the novice, meetings appear to be where the in-crowd gathers, where the corporate power brokers make big decisions behind a closed door. Once you begin going to meetings, you discover that you aren't allowed to just sit back and listen. Meetings are opportunities to show off your best corporate stuff; they may also be dangerous for the ill-prepared.

Special rules of etiquette apply to meetings both inside the company and at out-of-town conventions. You need to be aware of many things:

- How much participation is acceptable in each setting?
- When should you speak out with diplomacy, and when should you be blunt?
- Who is acting as leader of the meeting? Does that person always fill that role?
- What are the rules for conducting the meeting?
- How do behavior guidelines change when you represent your company out of town?

Whether you have attended many meetings or are about to discover what goes on behind the conference room door, be aware of how interactions change and how other people in the company respond in both kinds of meetings.

THE INTERNAL MEETING

Whether the meetings you attend are recurring or occasional, set a rule for yourself: Always plan to contribute something of value or to gain information that you can use to help your department. Only when you achieve such a goal is a meeting worth your time to attend.

This is also a point of etiquette. On the assumption that you are invited to meetings because you need to be there, you owe your company a contribution. You should become very uncomfortable if you go to a series of meetings and do not participate in some way; if that is the case, you are wasting time rather than using it well. That will affect your work as well as your self-esteem.

Your participation can take several forms. You may offer an opinion, support or disagree with someone else, or recommend actions to reduce expenses and increase profits. Or you could remain silent and then make changes in your department in response to information you gained at a meeting. Be aware that there are times to speak out and times to just sit silently and listen. Even when you are asked for an opinion, it is sometimes wiser to say as little as possible.

Example: You attend a meeting and plan to suggest a change in procedures. Your idea will save the company thousands of dollars a year. However, once the meeting starts, two other attendees raise another issue, and a heated debate follows. In that atmosphere, you decide to put off your idea until the timing is better. At one point, you are asked to give an opinion on the topic being debated. You give a brief answer, acknowledging that both sides have made valid points.

In this case, you delayed the agenda item you had in mind, recognizing that the timing was not good. Chances are, in that volatile moment, that you would not have had a fair hearing at any rate; so keeping silent was wise. In addition, you were asked to take sides in the debate. Rather than antagonize one person in favor of the other, you chose to give a diplomatic response, which was appropriate.

Another situation in which you are better off remaining quiet is when the leader does not want input. Meetings should be one of the most democratic exercises in the corporation—a chance for everyone to offer ideas and opinions, even when the chain of command is very specific and exact. However, some managers and executives use meetings not to encourage participation but to give speeches and impose their ideas.

Example: You attend a meeting to discuss plans for a six-month computer conversion. You have a number of ideas to present to make the conversation go smoothly in your department. However, the data processing manager (who called the meeting) does not ask for opinions or ideas. Instead, he runs down a list of what he wants from each manager. It becomes clear that the conversion will not involve teamwork. The meeting leader has a plan of his own; he only wants everyone to cooperate.

In this situation, you could try to offer your ideas at the meeting. However, you would be running up against the project leader, whose ideas of how to do the job do not involve participation. This is not a meeti..g in the sense of encouraging teamwork; it is an informational gathering. The leader imposed his schedule and want list but did not want or expect anyone to offer recommendations.

THE UNSPOKEN RULES

You have many opportunities to speak out, in meetings with many people, in one-to-one meetings, and in the reports, letters, and memos you write. You have probably heard the theory that behavior dealings should be conducted honestly and ethically. However, that may not be enough; you may have to use a measure of diplomacy that goes beyond basic behavior theory.

This is not to say that honesty and ethics must be thrown aside, only that you must occasionally temper your response to avoid embarrassing someone or creating an awkward situation. Honesty and ethics should be the standards by which we all act within the company, but how you time your response in some cases is essential. There is an unspoken series of rules you may need to be aware of. These may include the following:

1. *When you're asked for an opinion, that isn't necessarily permission to give it.* It could be a mistake to believe that, just because you have been asked to give your opinion, that's what is really wanted. The invitation to participate may be only a courtesy, or the person may really want to agree, whether you really do or not. If you are able to recognize the difference between a real desire for your opinion and one of the other cases, you are truly a diplomat. It's a matter of understanding the other person and knowing what he or she really needs and wants. On those occasions when you do speak out honestly, it might be prudent to offer criticism in the guise of a positive recommendation. This is a better approach than simply telling someone else you think he's wrong.

Example: During a meeting, the president asks you for your opinion concerning plans for rapid market expansion. The plan calls for 30 percent growth in sales during the next year. Your true opinion is that the planned growth is too rapid and that a slower course would be better and, ultimately, more profitable. You respond, "The plan itself makes complete sense, but I think there are risks. I suggest we consider scheduling it over more time, to ensure our profits and cash flow."

2. *Others may need to hear the truth, but they may not always like it.* You may find yourself in the difficult position of needing to offer observations or to disagree completely with someone. It may be impossible to soften your message. At those times, be prepared for a negative reaction. If you are correct, the other person will eventually recognize that fact, even if he or she resists it initially.

Example: The marketing director in one company designed a new product and convinced the president that it would be profitable. One manager disagreed and said so. For a month, the president did not invite that manager to weekly staff meetings, nor did he copy him on internal memos. Finally, though, the president realized the manager had spoken out with good motives—not to mention the fact that he'd decided the manager's argument was right.

3. *It is sometimes bad manners to say what is really on your mind.* It may be diplomatic to not respond specifically to a question posed during a meeting but to request a private appointment to convey your message—especially if you are compelled to contradict the meeting leader. For example, if the president of your company is completely wrong and you know it, and you want to say as much, consider getting together after the larger meeting.

Example: The president addressed managers during a weekly meeting he called his "task force." He had a new idea: to cut expenses by reducing the field service staff. You are aware that volume is on the rise and that customers expect continuing service after the sale. You say nothing but meet with the president after the larger meeting to express your concerns.

IDENTIFYING LEADERS

As a diplomatic meeting attendee, you need to choose and time statements carefully; you also need to be aware of who is in charge and what that means. On the surface, it may seem that the person who called the meeting, or the highest ranking attendee, is the natural leader. That isn't necessarily the case. Often the real leader in a meeting is not the one with title and rank but the attendee who acts in a leadership role, defines the meeting and sets its course, and motivates others to act and respond. The group might allow the titled leader to start the meeting and go from one agenda item to the next, but real leadership is more subtle than just monitoring the interactions.

When you identify the true leader in a meeting, remember this important rule of etiquette: Continue to respect the titled leader, and observe the rules of conduct.

Example: You attend a weekly meeting led by the vice-president of your division. He is indecisive and passive and seems unsure of how to arrive at firm decisions and a course for action. Another manager has taken over the role of leader and skillfully leads each agenda item to a logical conclusion. When you respond to statements or ideas, you make a point of directing your message through the vice-president.

This is a diplomatic and courteous way to proceed. You respond to the leadership of the meeting but also continue to observe the rule. Because you don't want the vice-president to sense that his authority is being bypassed, you and other attendees go through the motions.

Other rules of etiquette apply when you take the leadership role in someone else's meeting. This situation is an extreme test of your diplomacy. Your task is to lead other attendees through the agenda, arrive at decisions and assignments for action, and follow up after the meeting—all without appearing to take over the meeting from the rightful leader.

Here are some guidelines for handling this situation (also see Figure 6-1):

Figure 6-1. Guidelines: acting as unofficial meeting leader.

1. Always pose your ideas for action as recommendations, and never as orders.

2. Ask the leader questions that will lead to conclusions you need to implement.

3. Volunteer to take responsibility for any follow-up actions.

4. Report through the meeting leader.

5. Inform the meeting leader of all decisions and actions.

1. *Always pose your ideas for action as recommendations and never as orders.* You are completely justified in assuming a leadership role in meetings, even when someone else holds the title—assuming that the leader is not doing the job, and that other attendees accept you in that role. The final test: As long as the objectives of the group are being met, your leadership is appropriate.

However, remember that the titled leader is still sitting at the head of the table. Respect the position by offering a series of recommendations and by not taking all leadership away.

Example: You are acting as leader in a meeting. At one point, you want to ask another attendee to take on the assignment of writing a report. Rather than giving the assignment directly, you speak to the titled leader: "I recommend that you ask Bob to prepare a report on this and send copies to everyone present."

2. *Ask the leader questions that will lead to conclusions you need to implement.* A titled leader will sense a loss of prestige if the true leader takes over the reins of the meeting completely. With this in mind, you need to gently prod and even to place ideas in the leader's mind. In this way, you never impose your leadership on the group but proceed with diplomacy.

Example: A discussion centered on the question of methods for cutting costs in your division. You have concluded that another attendee needs to put a control system in place. You ask the meeting leader, "Should someone be given the task of taking action? Perhaps the controls we've been talking about should be put to work in the receiving department. What do you think?"

3. *Volunteer to take responsibility for any follow-up actions.* A true leader should conclude the meeting with a specific plan of action. Decisions should be made and put into effect, deadlines imposed, assignments given out. However, a weak leader won't know how to make the transition from talking about these ideas to delegating responsibility and then ensuring that the job gets done. You can fill in the void by volunteering to take follow-up actions.

Example: You have been able to recommend actions and delegation to attendees, all directed through the meeting leader. Now you need to ensure that the job gets done. You say to the leader, "While we were discussing the responsibilities, I listed them for you as an action plan. If you want, I'll be glad to coordinate the effort and report back to you on everyone's progress."

4. *Report through the meeting leader.* No matter how smoothly the process of leadership goes, remember that the person with the title is still the official leader. You need to keep that person involved, even if that involvement has no work-related significance as far as you and other

members of the team are concerned. You should continue reporting to the leader on every phase of action and follow-up.

Example: You are coordinating the efforts of other team members and making progress in completion of a project. The titled leader is not involved at all. However, you provide update reports each week, inform the leader of progress, and ask for guidance— knowing the whole time that you will be allowed to continue on the course you've set. Your interest is in getting the job done. But you're also aware that the leader must be kept involved, if only for the sake of appearance.

5. *Inform the meeting leader of all decisions and actions.* The point may arrive where you need to make a difficult decision. As a true leader, you will want to take responsibility and move forward. But as a diplomatic member of the meeting team, you also know that the leader has to be included.

Example: Your follow-up action has led you to a conclusion. You know the best course to take but need an executive decision before you can proceed. You consult with the meeting leader and explain the alternatives. You then ask for a decision. You may skillfully guide the leader to the obvious conclusion, but at the end of the discussion, the leader still believes he is in charge of the group and of the process.

If you proceed diplomatically, you can demonstrate respect for the position of leader and still assume an active leadership role for yourself. The passive leader may not be concerned so much with how the group perceives his role; he may be very possessive of the power and influence attached to the title.

GENERAL RULES FOR MEETINGS

Working as unofficial meeting leader demands energy and diplomacy, in addition to the usual work-related skills of the job. In comparison, observing the rules of conduct for meetings that are well-run and well-planned is a relatively easy task. Several general rules exist to help you get through the agenda in the time allotted, without interruptions and inefficiency. The rules for leading a meeting, which are summarized in Figure 6-2, include:

1. *Announce start and stop times in advance.* One way to limit the time you and others spend in meetings is to set a time limit. Announce the start time and the stop time, so that all attendees will know before they

Figure 6-2. Rules for leading a meeting.

1. Announce start and stop times in advance.

2. Observe the time constraints.

3. Take steps to minimize interruptions.

4. List agenda items in priority order.

5. Distribute the agenda in advance.

6. Set time goals for yourself for each agenda item.

7. Stick to the agenda and keep the meeting on the move.

come to the conference room how long they will be away from their departments.

2. *Observe the time constraints.* It is easy to say, "Start the meeting on time" but much more difficult to enforce that rule. For example, if half your attendees show up late, is it practical to start without them? If you need them at the meeting, you won't be able to proceed until they are there. So you may have to start late. However, you should still end the meeting at the scheduled time whenever possible, even if that means you don't get around to some of the agenda items.

3. *Take steps to minimize interruptions.* No meeting leader welcomes a string of interruptions, and you can take steps to deal with this annoyance. Tell employees in your department not to interrupt while your meeting is in progress. Hold the meeting in a room where you can close the door and get away from office traffic. If there is a phone in the room, disconnect it during the meeting. Some employees who would never enter a meeting room won't hesitate to make a phone call into the room if the line is working.

4. *List agenda items in priority order.* Take care of the most urgent business first, and leave less important topics for the end. In this way, priorities will be handled and the less urgent business can be deferred if time runs out. Also limit the number of topics to be covered in any one meeting, always assuming that discussion will require more time than you estimate.

5. *Distribute the agenda in advance.* Give attendees the chance to see what will be discussed well in advance of the meeting; if the attendees need to do any preparation, having the agenda will be essential. Of course, some critical meetings are called at the last minute, giving attendees no chance to prepare and leaving them with absolutely no idea of the purpose of the meeting. Effectiveness will be improved with a little planning.

6. *Set time goals for yourself for each agenda item.* Estimate the time you will need to cover each agenda item. This dictates the length of the total meeting and also gives you guidelines for leading others to summarize and make decisions. Only when you provide this leadership will you be able to avoid indefinite discussion and create the environment for constructive results.

7. *Stick to the agenda, and keep the meeting on the move.* Every leader needs to keep discussion on course and to make sure all agenda items are covered. Invariably, someone will raise issues not on the agenda. At that point, you need to gently but firmly bring the group back to the discussion. For example, you might say, "That's an important topic, but it should be covered at a different meeting. Let's go on to the next agenda item."

RULES FOR CONVENTIONS

The rules for attending and leading meetings change once you get on a plane and head out of town. At conventions, seminars, symposia, training courses, or sales meetings, you will face a number of issues you don't encounter in internal meetings.

Away from the watchful eye of the corporation, you need to be aware of these rules of behavior:

1. *If the company is paying for you to attend, it should get its money's worth.* Be aware of the company's financial investment in having you attend an out-of-town function. Even if you would have preferred not to go, attending such meetings is part of your job. Look for a way to demonstrate to the company that its investment was justified.

Example: You were sent to a three-day seminar for managers that dealt with methods for effective supervision. After you return, you write a report summarizing the key points covered in the seminar and distribute it to several executives and other managers. The purpose: to share information with others and to show management that you gained something worthwhile from the experience.

2. *Assume that everything you do will somehow get back to the company.* Personal behavior when you are out of town can affect your reputation and career. Guide yourself by the thought that, in some way, anything you do or say could get back to the company. Some people who are not accustomed to a lot of business travel drink more than usual, for

example, if only because they cannot sleep easily in a different time zone. Limit social activities out of town, recognizing that you represent your company while you are there.

Example: One manager, who had only limited travel experience, was sent 2,000 miles to attend an annual company convention. He tried to go to sleep at a reasonable hour, but could not. He missed his family and his routine and ended up in the hotel lounge. However, he drank only nonalcoholic beverages, knowing that he'd have to be at the meeting again at 8 A.M. and that drinking in this situation might appear to be unprofessional behavior.

3. *Attend all segments of the meeting unless you can justify not attending some parts.* Meeting attendance can be a chronic problem at out-of-town gatherings. If the meetings take place in locations with a lot of distractions, attendance at sessions tends to drop off each day, and some employees attend few, if any, sessions. Remember that when you represent your company, you have an obligation to attend all of the sessions, except those you can justify not going to.

Example: You attended a three-day convention last month and were present at almost all of the daily sessions. You did not attend one afternoon panel discussion, since it dealt with topics outside your area of expertise and interest. You justified this without any problem, but you were also prepared to report to management on what you gained from attending the rest of the convention.

4. *Not all of the productive work takes place during the sessions.* Some productive activities take place in social settings at out-of-town meetings. Because everyone there is away from home, it is not unusual for groups to meet for dinner, in a cocktail lounge, or on the tennis courts. These activities may be either strictly recreational or very business-related.

Example: You are a marketing manager working in the home office, and you attend a convention with branch office managers. After a day of sessions, you meet with several managers in the lounge. A number of issues are discussed informally, and you keep notes on the concerns they express and the promises you make. When you return home, you have a long list of actions that need to be taken.

Whenever you find yourself in a similar situation, be prepared to follow up when you return to the office. Even in a strictly social setting, affiliated members of your company may give you messages that should be delivered back in the office or ask you to follow up with information, or to respond in some other way. You have an obligation to respond to any requests that have been made of you.

Remember these guidelines:

1. *Keep notes.* No matter how social the environment, keep detailed notes on your conversations. You are at work even when you're sitting in a cocktail lounge with a branch manager. You need to remember the key points he or she raises and any responses you give.

2. *If you make promises, keep them.* When you return home, you should write a detailed report on all business-related discussions in which you participated at the meeting. This report should go to top management. Also be sure to respond promptly if you made any promises.

3. *Remember that you represent your company.* Be constantly aware that your statements and actions reflect on the company. Convey information very cautiously, and make sure you don't reveal anything that management does not want to get out. A branch manager may assume that everything you say comes directly from the president's mouth and that you are there as the representative of the company and its positions.

4. *Be careful when someone fishes for information.* Others may see an out-of-town social situation as a chance to get inside information on your company. If you sense that someone is trying to get the inside line, you should not say too much and keep opinions to yourself. Diplomatically avoid getting into discussions on topics not appropriate to the situation.

THE PROFESSIONAL APPROACH

For both internal meetings and out-of-town conventions, one rule of behavior always applies: You represent your department and your company. You expect a professional approach from others, and you should always set a professional standard of behavior for yourself.

If you separate personal and business pursuits, you will be able to survive meetings on all levels. For example, in an internal meeting, do not discuss personal interest, hobbies, problems, or activities. You are there to get through an agenda in a limited amount of time. During an out-of-town meeting, you may pursue personal interests—but company interests come first.

> **Example:** You attend a convention in a city you have never visited before, and you want to spend at least one day as a tourist. However, the convention agenda is very full. You arrive on Tuesday and sessions last through Friday evening. In order to avoid missing any sessions, you delay your departure until Saturday evening and use that last day to see the sights. You absorb the cost of the last day's hotel room as a personal expense.

If you attend an out-of-town convention and time is allowed in the schedule, you can take care of personal activities without breaking this rule. Some schedules allow a free afternoon so that the attendees can go off and enjoy some leisure time. In that case, you do not need to extend the trip but can use the free time any way you like. Some portions of the program might not be relevant to your professional interests, in which case you can use that time for yourself as well.

The rules of conduct in meetings are not difficult to master. If you understand your obligations and your priorities, you will be able to keep your commitment to the company and still achieve your own objectives.

A different type of meeting occurs over the telephone. However, because you don't see the other person and because the role of the telephone is so important in the company, a different set of rules apply. That's the topic of the next chapter.

WORK PROJECT

1. List and explain three guidelines to remember when acting as unofficial leader of a meeting.
2. Explain three rules to observe when leading an internal meeting.
3. What are the four guidelines for meeting with others out of town?

7

Telephones: Conducting the Invisible Meeting

If I take refuge in ambiguity, I assure you that it's quite conscious.

—Kingman Brewster

A manager had given an employee a copy of a very thick report published by the Department of Commerce to use in preparing a report.

"How's the research going?" the manager asked one morning.

"I'm having a lot of trouble getting information," the employee said. "I called the Department of Commerce to ask some questions and made a big mistake. I said I was trying to separate the wheat from the chaff."

"And what did they say?"

"Nothing. They transferred me to the Department of Agriculture."

The telephone, it seems, is all-powerful. Not only is it used to reach anyone and everyone; it can interrupt a closed meeting where a human being cannot get in. It demands a response, if only because the ringing is louder and more persistent than any person's voice and because you never know if an incoming call is from someone you need to speak to. If you are placing the call, invisibility can be an advantage; at the same time, it is easy for someone to avoid you or to delay speaking with you by screening calls.

By establishing sensible rules of etiquette for the use of the telephone, you can avoid creating the appearance of inefficiency or unavailability and, at the same time, maintain control over your schedule.

TELEPHONES AND MEETINGS

The telephone is indispensable. Person-to-person contact is not always practical or financially feasible, especially with so many organizations spread over large geographical areas. The telephone has enabled companies to expand physically without losing direct communication. However, this technological achievement, while a tremendous benefit, also has its disadvantages. Even when someone hundreds of miles away sounds close, the invisibility of the telephone changes the manners and attitudes of both participants in a conversation. It also affects the way we act in meetings.

Example: A manager receives a phone call from another department. While trying to listen to the caller, he continues working on a report on his desk. While the manager would never do this if the other person were in the office, the telephone makes it possible to forget the basic rules of good listening.

Example: A manager is holding an important meeting with an employee. During the half hour they are together, the manager spends nearly half the time on the phone. The manager has forgotten the basic rule of courtesy: A meeting should not be interrupted. The door is closed, so no one has come into the room, but the manager is easily reached by phone.

These are two of the most common mistakes involving the telephone and meetings. Manners change as a consequence of having a phone close at hand, and this change affects the way others perceive you. Everyone agrees that it's important to listen to others when they speak to us—whether the discussion takes place in person or over the phone. Most people would also agree that allowing interruptions during a meeting is poor form. Now ask yourself: Have you ever interrupted a meeting in your office to take an unexpected phone call?

Make two rules for yourself. First, listen with *all* of your attention when someone is speaking to you on the phone, just as if the person were in the room. Don't try to do two or more things at the same time. Second, when you are meeting with someone in person, don't allow the telephone to get in the way. Have your calls transferred or intercepted by someone else. Pay the other person the courtesy of your undivided attention.

Another important rule to observe: Don't grant a caller more influence than someone who is there in person. A common pitfall is to become victim to the phone lines at the expense of common courtesy. You can easily avoid this by recognizing the danger of the telephone.

Example: An employee showed up on time for an appointment with her manager, who was on the telephone. The manager waved the employee into her office but continued the conversation for another five minutes.

This situation probably wouldn't work in reverse. For example, if the manager were meeting with an employee and an unexpected call came through, would the manager ask the person to stay on the line for five minutes? Chances are the caller would take priority, even when the one-on-one meeting was scheduled for a specific time. There is a better and more considerate way to proceed.

Example: An employee arrives on time for a meeting with her manager. The manager is in the middle of a phone call. The manager ends the call quickly, explaining, "I have a meeting. Can I call you back in half an hour?"

In this example, the manager demonstrates respect for the employee. Rather than allowing the telephone to take precedence over a scheduled meeting, the phone discussion is deferred. A second step should be to redirect all incoming calls or to ask someone else to intercept them and take messages. Only then can the scheduled meeting take place without interruptions.

RECEIVING AND RETURNING CALLS

Conduct during meetings—in person or on the phone—is only one of the considerations for courteous and proper telephone behavior. You also need to set policies and standards for the way employees act on the phone and for receiving and returning calls.

> **Example:** You have a very busy, pressured schedule and spend a good deal of time away from your desk. As a result, there are a number of phone messages for you each day.

Set a rule for yourself that you will personally return every message you receive as soon as possible. If you cannot return a call the same day, ask someone else to at least call back and apologize for you. Also have the person give a precise time when you will return the call. Avoid letting a message remain unanswered. If someone is forced to call you a second time because the first message went unanswered, it's time to change your schedule.

If you are so busy that you cannot take the time to return calls, you need to set aside a specific time each day just to get back to everyone and to make your own calls. If you are unavailable to others, you will be perceived as disorganized or discourteous, or both.

The same standard should apply when you use an answering machine instead of having another person take your messages. Answering machines, like the telephone itself, are extremely convenient labor-saving devices. However, a number of people use them as screening devices and answer only selected calls. Answering machines remove human contact, which can become a negative—unless you diligently return all of your calls as soon as possible.

Return all of the calls received via your answering machine, preferably the same day. If you will be away from your department longer than one day, leave a message stating when you will return to your office and, if possible, including a phone number where you can be reached before your return.

Be aware of the tone in the message you leave in recorded form. You should sound professional, friendly, and interested in all of your calls. A poor quality tape in a business setting should be absolutely avoided. Put a lot of thought into what you will say and how you will say it. Prepare a script. Record it and then listen carefully. What impression does it make?

Keep promises made on the recorded message. If you say, "I will return your call later today," be sure you follow through. If you're not sure you will be able to get back to the person the same day, don't make the promise.

You may need to establish departmental standards for receiving and returning calls. Your company should create a policy and guidelines for everyone. However, few organizations take this important step; most company policies make rules covering only personal use. During business hours, personal use of the telephone is inappropriate and should be restricted. If an employee makes a long-distance call on a coffee break or lunch hour, the employee should charge the call to a credit card or a personal line or else reimburse the company. The larger issue concerning telephones is the impression you and the employees in your department make on outsiders. Beyond basic rules about personal use of the telephone, you may need to write down your own policies for taking messages, returning calls, and even for the way the telephone is answered. Without these guidelines, everyone in your department will answer the phone differently. And while some employees may be diligent about returning calls, others may not. Some employees, in the absence of specific rules, may even forget to write down messages for you or others.

DEPARTMENTAL PHONE RULES

Set guidelines for employees. Include these rules for telephone courtesy, which are also summarized in Figure 7-1:

1. *Take complete messages.* Employees taking telephone messages for you or for others in the department should write down the complete

Figure 7-1. Guidelines: employee telephone conduct.

1. Take complete messages.

2. State when the call will be returned.

3. Use the hold button carefully.

4. Answer the telephone professionally.

5. Give explanations when transferring calls to someone else.

message. Stationery stores sell carbonless sets for this purpose. It's a good idea to maintain a departmental record in the form of the second copy for possible later reference.

The message should include the caller's name, the time of the call, the person called, and a brief message, as well as a return telephone number and the best time to return the call. The message should also contain the time a return call was promised.

2. *State when the call will be returned.* Employees should be told to inform the caller when you will return to the department and when you will return the call. Be sure to honor the promise in all cases. If you are unable to call at the time stated, ask the employee to call for you, apologize, and defer the return call. Think of it as a promise to attend a meeting by telephone; just as you would let someone know when you are unable to come to a scheduled meeting, you should offer the phone caller the same courtesy.

3. *Use the hold button carefully.* Set rules for the use of the hold button. It should be used primarily to suspend a call while the employee

finds information needed for the conversation underway and as little as possible to field another call. Asking someone to hold because another line is ringing is irritating, although it may also be unavoidable. In any event, the first call should take priority. Ask the second caller for a phone number, and promise to call back immediately. Tell employees to avoid picking up the phone and saying only, "Please hold," then immediately parking the call.

4. *Answer the telephone professionally.* Each employee has an individual style for answering the phone. Some are formal, others very informal. Write down a policy for the appropriate method to use, whether employees are answering their own extension or someone else's. The best method is to identify the department or office and then to give one's name. For example, when answering your own phone, you might say, "Credit department, Angela Smith speaking." If someone else picks up your line, they might say, "Angela Smith's office, Bill Adams speaking."

5. *Give explanations when transferring calls to someone else.* No one likes calling one extension, only to be transferred to someone else. The more this occurs, the worse callers react. It might look as if everyone is passing the buck or simply as if people don't really know what they're doing. The worst situation of all is to be transferred a number of times, only to be left on hold at each station.

If employees in your department must transfer calls, have them follow these guidelines:

- When a transfer is necessary, apologize for the inconvenience and explain why someone else should handle the call.
- Never transfer a call without explanation.
- Give the callers the name of the person to whom they are being transferred, as well as the person's internal extension in case the call is disconnected during transfer.
- If your phone system allows, first call the other person and explain that you are transferring a call. Briefly fill the person in on the details before making the actual transfer.
- If the other person is not available, tell the caller you will leave a message and make sure the call is returned as soon as possible. Then take personal responsibility for ensuring that the other person does return the call.

Be aware that receiving a large number of messages may be a sign you're spending too much time away from the department. If your absences are unavoidable, be sure to return all calls within twenty-four hours.

SCREENING ETIQUETTE

Some messages are taken not because you are away from the department but because you cannot take the call or don't want to take it. For example, if you are in your office in a meeting, you should not allow interruptions. In this case, you might ask an employee to screen your calls for you.

Screening is necessary in a number of cases, if only because you need uninterrupted time to get through other tasks. However, you should set a personal rule: Never expect or ask an employee to lie for you, not even when it's the business-variety white lie.

There are two points that make this rule so critical. First, it sets a poor example for employees in your department. Second, even though many people consider a screening lie as acceptable practice, it simply isn't necessary.

Example: You need a full hour alone in your office to get through the interoffice mail and to complete a report promised to someone by this afternoon. You ask an employee to screen your calls. Instructions are to simply state you are unavailable and to promise the call will be returned within two hours.

The fact is, you are unavailable for telephone calls at that moment. If you take your calls when you need the quiet time, you will probably not be able to complete your work. You need to be able to manage time, including controlling the telephone.

How should your employees deal with the insistent caller? Will you leave it to their discretion whether to be firm or to put a call through? You should give employees precise guidelines, but also trust to their own judgment.

Example: You are in a meeting with a fellow manager and ask an employee to field your calls and take messages. However, you also state that if an emergency call comes through, you will take it. You will also take any calls from the president of the company, whom you phoned that morning. Since you are expecting a return call, you will interrupt your meeting if it does come through.

In this situation, it would be courteous to begin your meeting by stating, "I may receive a call from the president during our meeting." Then, if the call does come through, apologize and say, "I have to take this call."

When a meeting is interrupted by a call, state that you will keep it as short as possible—then make every effort to limit the conversation. For example, if the president calls, you may avoid a lengthy discussion by trying to set a time to meet or to call yet again and respond in greater detail. This technique is a form of self-screening. Just as you may ask an employee to take messages, you can keep essential calls to a minimum by deferring discussions until the ongoing meeting is through. Most people will understand and respond well when you ask them for a little more time, especially if you are in another meeting. In an extreme case, however, you may have to take another approach.

Example: During your meeting with another manager, the president of the company calls and your employee puts the call through to your office. You can see that the conversation will be a long one, and it cannot be deferred. So you ask the president to hold for one moment. You then explain the situation to the other manager, apologize, and ask whether the meeting can be continued a while later. You set a time and agree to meet in the other manager's department.

Rather than keeping the other person waiting while you are on the phone, you can use this technique to take care of the more urgent business first. You can then continue the face-to-face meeting when the crisis has passed. If the situation is handled with courtesy, the other person will understand and probably appreciate your consideration.

If you must take calls during a meeting, keep those calls on a strictly business level. Even though others might tolerate and understand the necessity of taking calls during a meeting, they will be frustrated if you spend several minutes in nonbusiness discussions. Keep the interruptions to a minimum whenever possible.

CRITICAL LISTENING

Conveying a message clearly is hard enough in person; on the telephone, the difficulty of achieving clear communication is increased tremendously. A large part of the message another person receives from you is nonverbal. Your tone of voice, facial expression, and body language all convey important information. On the telephone, these modalities for communicating are lost. Even tone of voice is distorted by phone lines, so that it becomes more difficult to interpret another person's words accurately.

You may create a poor impression without intending to, only because you are unaware of how you sound over the phone. Chances are you can recall incidents in which you gained an impression of someone else during a telephone conversation, only to finally meet the person and discover that your impression was completely wrong.

Be aware of your tone of voice and how well or how poorly you convey a sense of enthusiasm, both about what the other person is saying and how you feel about hearing from them. Some ideas:

1. *Ask employees for criticism.* If you are not sure of the impression you make on the telephone, invite a trusted employee to listen to your side of a conversation. Chances are your staff has already heard you and witnessed your telephone conduct. Accept any suggestions or criticisms. The purpose is not only to improve your style and tone but also to avoid any unintentional discourtesy to those on the other end of the line.

Example: A manager called his assistant into the office and explained, "I'm very uncomfortable on the telephone. To tell you the truth, I don't think I come across with a lot of confidence." The employee was glad to share an observation: "You say 'uh' and 'um' too much. It makes you sound unsure, even when you know your material." The manager realized this was true and began working on the problem.

2. *Record your own voice.* Turn on a tape recorder when you're on the telephone. You need only record your side of the conversation, which might be very revealing. Listen to your voice—the way you express ideas, the degree of enthusiasm in your voice, any verbal idiosyncracies such as using the same phrase too often. Improve your telephone style by avoiding the speech habits you find objectionable or distracting. If you do not convey enthusiasm, try to work on your voice modulation.

Example: A manager recorded her voice and noticed two things she wanted to change. First was her tendency to allow her voice to trail off at the end of sentences in which she offered opinions. This made her sound very uncertain. The second observation was that she began many sentences with the word 'actually.' This had become an unconscious habit, one she resolved to avoid in the future.

3. *Listen to others over the phone.* When you are speaking on the phone, listen very carefully to the way others speak and to their tone. What flaws do you hear? Does the other person sound unenthusiastic, disinterested, or even rude? Do you make similar mistakes? Be aware of how the telephone can misrepresent you and others, and learn from the mistakes you hear.

Example: A manager spoke frequently with an executive and noticed that rather than answering questions verbally, the executive tended to grunt. Although the executive was articulate and responsive in person, he had a poor telephone presence. In thinking about the impression this made, the manager realized that he too tended to do the same thing. As a result, he became much more aware of how a grunt affects others and of the poor impression it can make.

4. *Work to overcome flaws.* It is one thing to be aware of a flaw and quite another to correct it. Old habits are not easily overcome, and you

may need to work hard to change your style or tone. It might even be necessary to get someone else to help you.

> **Example:** A manager was aware that during telephone conversations, he tended to say 'yeah' rather than 'yes.' He asked a trusted staff member to help him by coming into his office while he made a phone call and to count the number of times he said 'yeah' during the conversation. He discovered that just having the employee in his office was a reminder of the problem. After three or four calls, he'd overcome the habit.

GUIDELINES FOR TELEPHONE CONDUCT

You will avoid the majority of errors in etiquette that involve the telephone by remembering this: Follow the same standards on the phone that you follow for attended meetings in person. This means avoiding interruptions, responding enthusiastically to others, and giving your full attention to the discussion at all times. It also means not allowing the telephone to override the rules of courtesy that apply to any meeting. Have your calls transferred and intercepted so that others do not have to sit through conversations that could and should wait. Never forget that the person in your face-to-face meeting has other tasks to do. That person's time is valuable; he or she deserves your respect and consideration and should not be expected to sit idly while you spend time on the telephone.

Make it clear to all members of your department that their telephone behavior should meet your standards and that the impression they make on others—whether customers, vendors, or employees in other departments—is largely created by their attitudes and actions on the phone.

A summary of the guidelines for telephone conduct appears in Figure 7-2.

Communication by telephone is made most difficult because of invisibility. Thus, you need to work harder to convey your message the way you intend. Another form of nonpersonal communication—correspondence—is equally challenging and involves special rules of etiquette as well. That's the topic of the next chapter.

Figure 7-2. Guidelines: telephone policies.

1. Always return phone calls.

2. Avoid telephone interruptions of meetings.

3. Listen carefully.

4. Screen calls honestly.

5. Use the hold button cautiously.

6. Be aware of how you sound.

7. Don't misuse answering machines.

8. Set departmental policies for answering the telephone.

WORK PROJECT

1. List and explain three of the guidelines for employees and telephone manners.
2. Explain the four ideas for improving your telephone style using critical listening techniques.
3. What are three general rules of etiquette for telephone conduct and communication?

8

Correspondence: Putting Your Mind on Paper

If you can't explain what you're doing in simple English, you are probably doing something wrong.

—Alfred Kahn

"Thanks for sending me a copy of your memo to the president," one manager said to another. *"I was very impressed. Most people wouldn't be willing to take such a big chance by putting their opinions in writing so strongly, especially when they criticize top management. It took a lot of guts."*

"I appreciate that, but I don't think you read the memo very carefully," the other manager replied. "I sent it under your name."

If you want to find out quickly whether someone has a professional attitude about his or her job, ask the person to write a memo. The result will demonstrate whether the person thinks clearly and expresses ideas well, is aware of the importance of the impression made by the written word, and is concerned about the appearance of documents he or she signs.

You have probably noticed that the style, content, and format of business correspondence are far from consistent. Some people present very neat, well-prepared reports or letters, while others produce sloppy work. People may not even be aware of the impression their written messages convey. The written messages you and the employees in your department send out do convey a very clear message about you. By being aware of the etiquette concerning the appearance and style of written messages and by carefully considering how you distribute correspondence, you will be able to create and maintain a positive image for your department.

CREATING AN IMPRESSION

The appearance and tone of correspondence tells the world all about you. They define professionalism and demonstrates the degree of care you have taken in the preparation phase; they also show whether you are aware of the etiquette involved.

A clean, precise, neat letter or memo tells other people that you are aware of appearances, that you care enough to take the trouble to make things right, and that you respect them enough to make the best possible impression. On the other hand, a letter full of misspelled words, erasures, thin margins, and poorly expressed thoughts conveys the opposite. Be aware of the basic rules for the preparation of business correspondence, which are listed below and summarized in Figure 8-1:

1. *Follow accepted formats.* The three forms of business correspondence—memos, letters, and reports—each have an accepted format to which you should conform as a matter of policy. Don't compound the communications problem by introducing new formats. You should deviate from this rule only if you want to try a better format. If your company's reports are in a format that is difficult to follow, you may want to propose a more efficient layout. Even then, you should be aware of the chain of command. Don't make the change until you have been given the go-ahead. If necessary, prepare your report in both formats, and put your ideas to the test. Similarly, if letters or memos are being prepared in an unacceptable business format, you may tactfully suggest

Figure 8-1. Checklist: basic correspondence rules.

1. Follow accepted formats.

2. Be aware of first impressions. Neatness does count.

3. Check spelling thoroughly, especially for names.

4. Edit with the goal of reduction.

5. Write in a clear style.

6. Never let unacceptable material leave the department.

companywide standards and guidelines that will make a better impression.

2. *Be aware of first impressions. Neatness does count.* A neatly prepared memo or letter makes a very good impression and is usually more credible to others than a careless one. You may be the absolute professional in your attitude, clarity of thought, and motivation, but if your correspondence lacks professionalism, others may have a difficult time believing you think clearly and may assume you are as disorganized as your correspondence appears to be.

If only as a matter of courtesy, make it a goal for all of your correspondence to have a completely professional appearance. Apply this standard to yourself and to the employees in your department.

3. *Check spelling thoroughly, especially for names.* If you prepare written material on a word processing system, checking spelling is a relatively easy routine, involving one or two keystrokes. If you are still

writing memos, letters, and reports manually, you may ask someone else to check your typed draft for any spelling errors. Then check the final copy yet again. Everything you send out should be subjected to a spelling check beforehand.

This rule is particularly important when other people's names are involved. Never misspell someone else's name, especially when your memo or letter is addressed to him or her. That suggests that you weren't concerned enough to take the trouble to check the spelling in the company directory before writing your letter or memo.

4. *Edit with the goal of reduction.* A first draft is rarely the best possible version of the message you want to send out. Editing business correspondence is not difficult if you take the approach that an idea can always be expressed in *fewer* words—a two-page letter will be clearer when the same message is reduced to one page, a lengthy paragraph in a memo may be taken down to two or three lines, and a long report may work better as a shorter one. Adopt the attitude that the reader of your correspondence must use his or her time economically; the shorter you write, the better. In some cases, the less said, the better.

5. *Write in a clear style.* If an idea can be expressed in a short sentence, avoid using a longer one. If a one-syllable word suffices, avoid the four-syllable word. Be aware of the length of sentences, avoiding the run-on. You do not need to make a message sound important; important messages come across best with simple language. Also watch the rhythm in your writing style. If all of your sentences are about the same length, the reading will be tedious and uninteresting. Vary sentence length; refresh your reader with brief paragraphs and a readable, friendly rhythm.

Some businesspeople write in a very technical and impersonal manner. Your writing will be perceived as better and more professional when you avoid this common error.

6. *Never let unacceptable material leave the department.* Set a rule for your department: No material may be sent without first being reviewed for content, tone, style, spelling, and neatness. There are two reasons for this rule. First, you want to create the best possible impression. Second, as a courtesy to the reader, you want to make your message as clear and as professional as possible. You do not have to review each and every memo or letter prepared by subordinates. Delegate the review process within the department, having employees provide cross-review for one another.

WHAT TO PUT IN WRITING

Like the telephone, written correspondence makes communicating ideas more difficult. You naturally want to minimize the volume of paperwork in your department, since preparing documents takes up time and the finished work occupies filing space. However, when messages must be conveyed in writing, remember that clarity and content define the difference between a good letter or memo and an unacceptable one.

You already know how difficult it is to carry on a dialogue on the telephone. Without the benefit of seeing the other person's body language, facial expression, and other reactions, you need to express your ideas in a manner different from that you use when you are in the same room as your listener. When you write, you are even farther removed from the other person. On the telephone, at least, you get immediate feedback. You can tell by tone of voice and statements how the other person is reacting. With correspondence, you do not have this limited but useful feedback. Therefore, you need to take great care to ensure that you do not write anything that could be misunderstood. Demonstrate that you are aware of the difficulty in communication and that you respect the other person enough to express your ideas clearly.

Example: The manager of the Eastern marketing department sent a memo to the manager of the Western marketing department to announce a meeting the following day. In part, the memo read, "I will expect you to present a verbal report on your department's progress to date." The response? The Western marketing manager phoned and angrily protested the "attitude" of the Eastern manager.

The writer's intention had been not to force the other manager to account for activities in his department but to invite attendance and participation at the meeting. However, her selection of words in the memo conveyed a different idea. Be aware of how your words might sound to someone else.

Example: The manager in the previous example could have taken a different approach. Starting out with a brief explanation of the purpose of the meeting, she could have included an invitation to take part. The wording could have been: "I will be presenting a brief verbal update on progress to date in the Eastern division. Can you attend and cover the same information for Western? Your participation will be appreciated."

In this message, the request is reworded so that the reader does not feel intimidated or insulted. The first version sounds like an attempt to place the reader in a subordinate position; its message could be perceived as, "It's *my* meeting. You *will* be there. You *will* give a report." Which was not the manager's intention.

Deciding what message to send and how to phrase it is difficult. But as long as you are aware of the etiquette involved, you will stay on course. Apply the same rules you would use in a one-on-one conversation. You know that there is an appropriate way to communicate a message and an unlimited number of ways in which you can cause a misunderstanding. From trial and error, you learn how to communicate in person. Achieving the same end result in writing may be more elusive; however, with practice, you can acquire the skill.

Written communication has one benefit that you don't have in person: You have a second chance, and even a third or fourth chance, to fix the problem before the other person even sees your words. Avoid misunderstandings by using the editing process. Some guidelines:

1. *If you're having a problem deciding how to express an idea, put it aside for a while.* Don't punish yourself by trying draft after draft for a memo or letter. The harder you try, the more frustrating it all becomes. When you are having a problem, put the work aside for a while. Work on something else and come back to it later. The breathing space might be just what you need to figure out the best way to express yourself.

2. *Ask someone else to review your work.* You can ask an employee, a friend, or another manager to look over your draft and make suggestions. Having a trusted editor at hand could be your best weapon in your quest to improve your written communication—as long as any criticism is given fairly and accurately and as long as you are able to take good advice when it is offered.

3. *Don't put especially difficult messages in writing at all.* Some messages are too sensitive or require too much diplomacy for you to tackle

them in writing. Remembering that written communication is the most remote form of communication, you might be better off dealing with some issues in person. Recognize the problems inherent in relying on written communication, and avoid the difficulty altogether by arranging a face-to-face meeting instead.

4. *If there is a misunderstanding, ask for a face-to-face meeting. Resolve the problem without delay.* There will be occasions when reaction to your message—no matter how well written—will be negative. In these cases, immediately meet with the other person. Apologize for the misunderstanding. Defuse the problem before it accelerates, and explain the message you intended to send.

WHAT NOT TO PUT IN WRITING

One unspoken standard that applies to business correspondence is: Never express anything in writing that you might want to reverse later. Put another way, never put words on paper that you might regret. This rule probably should apply to all writing, personal or business. However, in a business situation, you need to be aware of the potential for political consequences that might arise from saying too much or from expressing thoughts or emotions you don't want etched permanently in the "cultural memory."

Example: A manager was involved in an ongoing conflict with the manager of another department. He wrote a memo complaining about the situation, disputing several actions the other manager had taken over the past month. It was a very angry and confrontational memo. The problem was resolved eventually through a series of compromises and personal meetings. However, even after the resolution, the then-famous memo occasionally came up in conversation. The manager realized—too late—that expressing his anger in writing had been a serious error.

You should also avoid putting in writing anything of a highly confidential or sensitive nature. Some highly confidential matters must be documented, of course. However, there are appropriate methods for this, such as hand-delivering a memo concerning an employee reprimand to a personal file. In such a case, no one but the manager and the employee has a right to see the memo; sending it by intracompany mail could lead to problems if it were misdirected.

If you have to discuss sensitive information with someone else, a face-to-face meeting is preferable. You may document your position and make notes about the meeting with a "memo to the file," which should be kept locked up. If you are asked to put your suggestions, observations, criticisms, or complaints in writing, be sure to protect the writing information carefully. However, sensitive information need not involve personnel issues or complaints. A seemingly innocent recommendation can create problems if put into written form. It can also violate the rules of behavior in your corporate culture, even when you do not intend to break those rules. Be aware that an innocent memo could become a political sore point in the future.

Example: One organization's home office served as a coordination point for three separate corporations owned by the same stockholders. The marketing department manager wrote a memo to the president recommending centralization of administrative services, which were separate for each company. The idea would have reduced expenses and was offered with the best motives. The president read the memo and put it aside for several months. When the company's chief accountant came up with the same idea several months later, the president pulled out the marketing department manager's detailed memo and gave the accountant a copy. The accountant saw the memo as an inappropriate idea to come from marketing, and he confronted the manager with a difficult question: Why did *you* write this memo in the first place, and why didn't you send me a copy?

There might not be a simple or logical answer in this situation, other than to admit the oversight. The marketing manager could have kept the ideas private, expressing them to no one—a safe alternative, but not an acceptable solution to a manager whose motivation is to reduce company overhead. If the accounting manager had been approached with the idea, his reaction might have been the same: hostility. If the marketing manager had broached the idea verbally, the president might not have remembered it or might have asked for a written summary of the proposal, leading to the same outcome.

The problem is a cultural one. A territorial manager sees ideas from outsiders as invasions and feels threatened by them. The cultural rule that was broken in this case was not the expression of the idea. That was proper and appropriate. It was failing to include the accounting manager in the correspondence chain. The marketing department manager could have easily written the memo to the president *and* the accounting manager jointly, or at least, sent a copy of the memo to the accounting manager.

FORMATTING RULES

Considering the volume of written material produced in companies, it is surprising that few companies have written policies dictating the formatting rules to be used consistently by all employees. Letters sent to customers, vendors, and others outside the organization make a definite impression, whether positive or negative. In many cases, critical messages are prepared and sent in a format dictated not by policy but by the individual who types or processes it.

You can follow the etiquette of business correspondence for yourself and in your department and may be able to influence the entire organization by your example and by recommending guidelines for written communication. The major problem you will encounter in instituting change will be convincing decision makers that correspondence is important enough to justify the effort required to establish and enforce standards.

Some suggested guidelines that you can put into place, at least on the departmental level:

1. Memos should include the date, the name of the recipient or recipients, and the name of the sender. Be sure to use the full names and, when appropriate, the titles of recipients. The memo may be spaced according to your own preferences; however, 1.5 or 2-space format is

easier to read than single spacing. Allow generous margins left, right, and at the bottom of each page.

2. Letters should be formatted with a full inch margin left and right. The bottom margin should also be an inch from the edge of the paper, unless your company's letterhead includes printed matter at the bottom, in which case the margin should be one inch from the printed matter.

3. Paragraphs should be indented five to ten spaces. Alternatively, you can leave one extra line at the end of each paragraph and eliminate indenting, except for outline-form information in the body of the letter.

4. Second pages of memos and letters should include the date and page number at the top.

5. Salutations are used only in letters, not in reports or memos. A formal letter should be addressed to Mr. or Ms. in most instances; for business letters to peers, immediate supervisors, or others you know well, you may use first names in the salutation. However, the name should be expressed in formal style in the name/address section at the top of the letter.

6. Reports should be formatted consistently from one period to another; reports with similar subject matter should also follow an accepted format. The report should enable the reader to find the most critical information quickly. A summary page briefly describing the report, major points, and conclusions is helpful to busy readers who may want only those highlights. Assume that recipients will not always read the entire report and may appreciate a helpful summary. All information in the body of the report should be cross-referenced so it can be found easily.

7. All business correspondence should be typed or printed out. A note (as opposed to memo or letter) may be handwritten. Reports should never be sent in handwritten form, although some supplementary material may be. (For example, a financial report might be supported with a photocopy of a worksheet.) Envelopes should always be typed, except when you use interoffice transmittal envelopes within the company.

The formats you select for memos, letters, and reports should be used consistently. Ensure that employees follow the guidelines you specify, and institute a procedure for cross-editing and spell-checking among your staff. If you use the services of a word processing or typing pool, you have the right to specify a preferred format, even if it is not used on a companywide basis.

With the widespread use of word processing, acceptable formats for departmental use can be stored in the system and used with little trouble by employees. If an employee prefers to store a draft in one format, rearranging it into another is a relatively simple procedure. Your guidelines or departmental rules can also be stored in the system, so that they are immediately available to anyone writing memos, letters, or reports.

DISTRIBUTING COPIES OF MATERIAL

Rules of etiquette apply to sending copies of written material. When you write a letter, memo, or report and submit it to one or more departments or individuals, you may need to also copy others who are not directly involved

Some guidelines:

1. *Send copies to everyone who is mentioned in the memo or letter or whose area of responsibility will be affected.* It is a courtesy to keep others informed when their names or departments are mentioned in any business correspondence. This is especially important when a decision will affect the other department. Avoid offending other managers by failing to keep them advised. Even if the document is not read, you protect your own position by ensuring that a copy was sent.

Example: You sent a memo to the vice-president in response to her request for ideas for cutting expenses. In the memo, you mentioned a monthly procedure affecting your department and two others. The managers of the other two departments also received a copy of your memo.

2. *If in doubt, send a copy.* It is better to send too many copies of correspondence than to send too few. Some people think it bad manners

to be left off the distribution list, even when the subject matter is not of concern to them.

Example: You sent a copy of a memo to all the middle managers in your company except two. Your reasoning: They were not affected by the topic in the memo. However, when they discovered they'd been left out, both reacted poorly and asked to be included in future distribution lists.

3. *List the names of everyone to whom a copy was sent.* Whenever you send a copy of a letter, memo, or report to a number of people, all the recipients' names should be listed on each copy. For letters, the notation is made beneath the signature block. For memos, the names are listed at the top if the memo is addressed to the distribution list collectively; if the memo is sent to only one person, those who receive copies should be listed at the end. A report's distribution should be specified in the cover letter or on the first page of the report.

Example: The president asked you to prepare a report including recommendations for changes in procedures. As part of your work on the report, you asked other managers for their ideas. When the report was sent, you submitted copies to each manager, as well as to your immediate supervisor. All of their names were included on the front of the report.

4. *Send blind copies very selectively.* In isolated cases, you may want to send a copy of correspondence to someone without letting the recipient know you are doing so. This is called a "blind" copy, since the person to whom the correspondence is addressed does not know someone else received a copy, too. The blind copy should be used very carefully and with great discretion, and the person receiving the blind copy should be informed that it is blind, so that the action will be kept confidential. There are limited instances in which sending blind copies is appropriate.

Example: You asked a fellow manager for help in writing a difficult letter. The manager asked you for a copy of the final version.

Even though there was no business need for her to see the letter, you sent a blind copy as a courtesy.

Example: You received a solicitation from a vendor and wrote back, explaining that your company was under contract with one of their competitors. A blind copy was also sent to your contact in the existing vendor company. Your purpose: To demonstrate your compliance with the terms of the contract, as well as an appropriate loyalty to the vendor.

FOLLOWING UP ON CORRESPONDENCE

Whenever you correspond with someone else, you take on an obligation. A letter or memo is only the initiation of a dialogue and is rarely the concluding step. This point is often overlooked in the corporation, where many letters and memos go unanswered.

The obligation to respond to correspondence involves one of two follow-up steps. If you offer an idea or volunteer to take a specific action, you are obligated to come through. And if you ask the other person to respond, you are also obligated, this time to ensure that response does come; when it does, you will probably need to work with the other person in a cooperative effort to achieve the desired end result.

With these points in mind, follow these guidelines for correspondence:

1. *End the message with a specific question or request.* End your letters or memos in a way that is likely to lead to action on the other side. Don't merely let your discussion end passively; give the other person a reason to answer.

Questions are the most effective means for prompting a response. For example, if you need to meet with the other person, end with, "When will it be convenient for you to meet?" If you are offering to prepare a report, ask, "Would you like me to prepare this report for you?" The question deserves an answer. In comparison, if you explain your position but let the letter end without the question, you are less likely to receive a response.

2. *Offer or suggest a response deadline and an action deadline.* It also helps the other person when you suggest deadlines. Without a specific date, it is too easy to put off acting or even responding to a written message. For example, you might write to another manager and ask for a face-to-face meeting. End with the question, but also suggest a specific date: "Can we meet before this Friday? That will give us time to complete the job by the following Wednesday." This question/statement provides two deadlines, one for a response and another for follow-up action.

3. *If you make any promises, be prepared to keep them.* The appearance, language, and tone of your message make distinct impressions on others. However, nothing is remembered as well as a kept promise—unless it's an unkept one. If you make any promises in your correspondence, be absolutely certain that they are kept. Promises should include a proposed deadline you know you can meet. If the deadline is accepted, keep the promise, without exception. If a new deadline is offered in response, make every effort to honor it, or explain why it is not possible to do so.

4. *If you do not receive a reply, telephone or visit the other person.* You deserve the courtesy of a reply, even if it says only, "I haven't had the chance to read your memo. I will get back to you with an answer within three days." However, many memos and letters are not answered promptly, or at all. In those cases, you have the right to ask for a response, even if that means visiting in person and asking for a meeting. Some people will willingly take half an hour to speak with you but can't seem to find ten minutes to reply in writing.

Correspondence makes a first impression, defining you and your department professionally. In a similar manner, your personal appearance makes a statement and can affect both your career and your reputation. For example, a highly efficient manager will not be perceived as efficient if he or she doesn't also dress the part. The etiquette of personal appearance in the corporate culture is the topic of the next chapter.

WORK PROJECT

1. List and explain three of the basic correspondence rules.
2. What are four methods for editing your work to improve communication?
3. Explain the four rules to follow when preparing and sending out copies.

9

Dress Code: Fitting in With Style

A fair exterior is a silent recommendation.

—Publilius Syrus

An employee asked his manager for advice on how to dress at work. The manager suggested, "A little variety might help. Perhaps you need to make a fashion statement."

The next day, the employee showed up at work wearing the same outfit as the day before, but with one change. There was a large pin on his lapel. It read, "My other suit is in the cleaners."

Blue jeans, tennis shoes, casual shirts—depending on where you work and the region of the country, these may be taboo in your office or they may be the uniform of the day.

The rules for dress are unique to every company. Whether very strict or very loose, the business fashion rules by which you live are based on a single idea: conformity. Even those who resist the idea of going along with the crowd agree that career success often depends on not standing out in the crowd. The successful manager does not draw attention to clothing but conforms to the generally accepted rules in the corporate culture. The idea of conformity arouses resistance in our minds; however, when you're interested in moving up the corporate ladder, conformity in dress is essential.

If your wardrobe draws the attention of others, you have violated the unspoken rules. That may mean dressing too poorly for the situation—or it could mean going too far in the other direction and dressing too well. Both fashion statements violate the rule: In the organization environment, you dress for success by not drawing attention to the *way* you dress.

DECIDING HOW TO DRESS

In today's social and business culture, traditional beliefs and generalizations concerning "appropriate" rules of dress are being abandoned. A company's rules often break with tradition. You may need to observe different dress codes for different employers, for different jobs, or even when you are transferred from one branch office to another.

Example: A home office employee of a company based in New York wore a suit to work each day. When he was transferred to the Southern California office, he soon discovered that sports coats were usually the maximum in dressing up. Most employees rarely even wore a tie.

Example: One prospective candidate was preparing for a job interview with a local conservative bank. He put on an exceptionally loud tie. A good friend advised that, since the job was in a conservative institution and involved financial responsibility, a softer, quieter tie would be more appropriate.

Frequently, the generalizations made about dress codes apply to companies grouped in a single region, particularly large cities. These "rules" include statements such as:

- Those in conservative occupations (banking and finance, for example) should *always* dress conservatively.
- Every man should have four suits. Every woman needs at least fourteen business outfits (or ten, or twenty-three).
- Women must always wear dresses or skirts and never come to work wearing pants.

The rules that really apply depend on a number of factors, including the dress code that is actually observed in your particular workplace, the region of the country, the season, and your personal clothing budget.

Abandoning rigid beliefs and generalized rules for dress, what guidelines should you employ in your job? The way you dress will affect your career, but this does not mean that only the best-dressed will be promoted. It does mean that fitting in, or conforming, is more likely to lead to success than making a different or distracting fashion statement.

The easiest way to decide how to dress on the job is by observation. Watch what others wear. What makes a favorable impression on you, and what do you find distracting or inappropriate? Some people wear ill-fitting clothing or lack variety in their wardrobe. Others draw attention to themselves by out-dressing everyone else. Both statements— wearing poorly made, dull clothing or dressing flamboyantly—are inappropriate in your company. The individual who fits in well—in other words, whose clothing is not really even noticed—has found the middle ground that clears the way for career success.

It is not difficult to create a wardrobe that conforms to the middle ground rule, nor is it expensive to maintain. However, budget is a very important and often limiting factor. If you are barely able to match income and expenses now, spending money on a business wardrobe will be a low priority. Some solutions:

- Look for affordable, well-tailored clothing. You do not need to spend a lot of money to dress comfortably and appropriately, even in the most formal office.
- Buy clothing on the time payment plan. Use store credit cards or bank cards that allow you to make partial payments each month. Build a clothing allowance into your personal budget.
- Build your business wardrobe gradually over time. You do not have to replace your current wardrobe in a single shopping spree.
- Add variety to your professional wardrobe by including well-chosen accessories. Having separate pieces that can be combined for a finished look reduces the need to spend a large amount of money for your wardrobe (and the need for a lot of closet space).

Inappropriate dress can inhibit your career. If peers and supervisors perceive you as someone who does not know how to dress in the professional environment, they may conclude that you are not a serious candidate for promotion. Be aware of these generalized, but often true, points:

- Ill-fitting, poorly-made business outfits are the mark of inexperience and are associated with those new to the business scene or those who have not yet discovered the importance of appearance.
- Comfortable, high-quality clothing is seen as the mark of success, even when the statement that clothing makes is very soft and quiet.
- Out-of-style dress is often seen as the sign of obsolescence. Others may subconsciously associate your personal dress code with the way you think.
- Excessively expensive, high-fashion, or loud clothing is perceived negatively. Coworkers often view overdressed people as insecure or insensitive to the business environment.
- People will label you on the basis of your personal appearance. If you dress and groom yourself carelessly, you may be perceived as careless or disorganized or as a liberally minded person in a conservatively minded company.

INFORMAL ATTIRE

In some business situations, informal attire is both appropriate and acceptable. However, there is a big difference between casual and sloppy dress. When you dress in casual attire, you still need to be aware of fit, appearance, color combinations, and the quality of design. You can appear sloppy whether you're dressed to the hilt or wearing weekend clothing.

If you are invited to a function away from the office and you're not sure what dress is appropriate, don't be embarrassed to ask. That's better than guessing and then showing up dressed inappropriately.

Example: You received an invitation to a company dinner at the president's home. This is an annual event, but you have been with the company less than one year, so this is your first invitation.

It will take place at 4 P.M. next Saturday. At first, you assume that a coat and tie will be appropriate. However, when you ask, you are told it will be a barbeque and you are expected to dress informally.

Example: Your company hosts an annual Christmas dinner at a local banquet hall. You assume that the appropriate dress will be a coat and tie; however, you are also aware that the occasion might be very formal. You check with your immediate supervisor, who confirms your first assumption.

It would have been a mistake in this example to show up in either casual dress or black tie or gown. It is always best to ask, even if the answer seems obvious. It would be embarrassing to arrive at a company function and discover you're the only one dressed incorrectly for the occasion. Remember, it's not easy playing lawn tennis in a tuxedo.

GUIDELINES FOR WARDROBE SELECTION

Follow these guidelines for selecting your corporate wardrobe:

1. Be aware of regional customs. In large urban areas, where the majority of people work, business suits are most often appropriate. In some regions, however, informality is the rule; in Florida, the South, and the Southwest, for example, company dress codes are often very informal, although in certain industries or corporations, they are quite formal. A lot depends on the company itself.

Example: The marketing director of a multi-branch corporation frequently met with customers and branch managers out of town. He discovered that the corporation's sales employee observed traditional dress for business meetings; however, in some regions, customers showed up to luncheons and even dinner meetings in casual dress.

2. The rules may change with the season. This goes beyond the summer and winter styles. In regions of extreme temperature change, for example, ties and coats may be abandoned in the hotter months.

Example: A manager of a corporation based in New York spent several months in two branch offices, one in the southern part of Florida and the other in Hawaii. In both locations, dress codes were relaxed in the middle of the hot season. Employees came to work in loose-fitting, casual clothing rather than in more traditional outfits.

3. Personal appearance and body type may limit wardrobe variety or provide opportunities for different dress style. Some popular styles will not compliment you. If your weight changes, you may need to alter or replace the wardrobe that was comfortable and appropriate last year. Some people can get away with wearing loose-fitting popular styles, while others do not feel or look right in the same clothing. For example, a very thin manager may have trouble finding well-fitting clothing and may need to have tailored not only his suits but his shirts and slacks as well.

4. Work within your personal budget, and avoid going into debt just to meet the unspoken rules. Your wardrobe is an important investment in your career, but you need to balance the desirability of an attractive and professional wardrobe with the realities and limitations of your budget.

Example: A manager on a very restricted budget spent money to build and maintain a professional wardrobe. Because of financial limitations, she used a revolving charge card and budgeted monthly payments, rather than attempting to pay for every new outfit in cash.

Your need for a professional wardrobe will also be affected by the nature of the job itself. If you have a low-visibility job, you may be able to get away with a less formal, less expensive wardrobe. However, if you are expected to attend a number of meetings each week or to meet with your company's customers on a regular basis, you will need to invest more money in your wardrobe.

Example: A manager of a back office department rarely attended meetings or left the office for outside contact, so he was able to manage with a limited wardrobe. Another manager at the same earnings level attended an average of three meetings per week and also met frequently with customers. His wardrobe requirements were more demanding.

Be aware of your clothing, and observe the rules of common sense, not only in the style and selection of fabrics but in accessories as well. For example, both men and women should avoid wearing an excessive amount of jewelry in the office. Color combinations and styles should not be so loud that they draw attention. Most business settings tend to the conservative when it comes to style.

Examples: A man's tie should be soft and coordinated with the colors and styles of shirt and suit. If a man expects to take off his jacket in the office, he should avoid short-sleeve shirts. He should always wear a jacket at meetings and at business meals. A woman's accessories should not distract others or make a loud statement. A woman's clothing style, including jewelry and accessories, should be appropriate for the professional environment.

GETTING HELP IN SELECTING YOUR WARDROBE

If the unspoken dress code in your company is difficult to understand, you may need to seek help with your wardrobe. Consider these sources:

1. Observation is always the best way to learn. Base your wardrobe standards on the rules someone else observes. Find another employee whose wardrobe makes the statement you would like to make. What is it about that person and his or her style that you admire? Perhaps the person's attire conveys a sense on professionalism or is understated in a stylish way. It may be that the wardrobe creates an image of self-confidence or ease. When you observe others, you might have to look for the less than obvious; it may be that the least noticeable person is making the best possible statement.

2. Many clothing stores employ fashion consultants who are available to customers. Speak with the consultant, explain the goal you are trying to reach, and begin a program of gradual wardrobe replacement. If the consultant understands that you want to make a very low-key fashion statement, he or she will be able to steer you to clothing that achieves your objective. If the store does not have a consultant, work with a salesperson who is willing to take time to help you, beyond just making the sale and ringing it up.

3. Check popular magazines—not just the high-fashion, style-conscious ones, but also the business and professional magazines. Look at the ads and make your own judgment about the fashion statement a particular style makes. Imitate the statement you consider appropriate by seeking clothing of similar cut, color, and style.

4. Speak with friends and business peers. You may be on good terms with a fellow manager who dresses well. Ask that person where he or she shops for clothing, and then check the same store on your own. Ask trusted friends or relatives for advice, especially those who seem to have a good, balanced fashion sense without needing to make a loud statement.

If you receive an unexpected promotion, you may need to replace your wardrobe and change the statement you make in short order in order to make the right impression.

Example: A manager with a modest, acceptable business wardrobe was promoted to a new position that involved a high degree of customer contact. She was scheduled to start in the new job in one week. Realizing that the high level of public contact demanded a different professional image, she immediately visited a moderately priced store and began planning an upgraded wardrobe. In order to complete this task quickly, she selected a store where the salespeople were both knowledgeable and helpful.

GROOMING GUIDELINES

Closely connected to the dress code is your company's unspoken grooming code. In virtually every company, as in all sectors of society, certain minimum requirements, including the basic rules for creating a clean, neat appearance, exist. Here are some guidelines:

1. Men should always come to the office clean-shaven. They should shave every morning and never appear in the office with a day's growth of hair, no matter how slight. A moustache or beard should be kept at reasonable length and should be well-trimmed at all times.

2. Wear hair at an acceptable length. Men's hair should be kept off the collar and the ears. A woman's hair should be maintained at or above the shoulder. These generalizations, of course, vary with personal preference and custom.

3. Both men and women should wear fragrances in moderation. Avoid especially noticeable aftershaves, colognes, or perfumes. A subtle statement is preferred.

4. Fingernails should be uniform in length and kept clean. Women should avoid all but conservative nail color, if they wear any at all. Hands are always in sight, and others form impressions based on their appearance and cleanliness and the length of nails.

5. Makeup should be worn very carefully. Too much makes a poor impression; a very small amount achieves the intended effect: highlighting natural features rather than hiding them.

6. Grooming chores—makeup, hair care, and fingernail care—should not take place in view of others. Perform your grooming chores while on a break, not while on the office floor itself.

7. Be ready for emergencies. Keep a small sewing kit in your office, so you can make minor repairs as necessary. If you are called suddenly to attend a meeting and, at the same moment, a button comes off your coat, you need to replace it on the spot. A quick sewing job is better than the alternatives: showing up with a missing button or improvising a repair.

Most rules of dress and grooming are based on common sense. However, it is easy to forget this and to become caught up in the misconception that an exceptional statement is demanded or necessary. Avoid the temptation to compete with others. Imitate soft statements that convey a highly professional image.

Dress code guidelines are summarized in Figure 9-1. They can help you dress appropriately, regardless of your particular position in the corporation.

Simply being aware of dress codes, as unspoken as they are, is most of the battle. Pay attention to how others dress and groom. Just as all

Figure 9-1. Checklist: dress code guidelines.

1. Learn mainly from observation.

2. Balance personal comfort and career considerations.

3. Alter your wardrobe for the region and the season.

4. Avoid making an excessive fashion statement.

5. Invest in high—quality, practical clothing.

6. Be aware of your company's unspoken dress code.

7. Use common sense and moderation in selection of jewelry, accessories, and fragrances.

8. Follow the basic rules of good grooming.

forms of behavior are made acceptable as the result of common practice, the dress code rules in your company are dictated by what is thought to be "normal." And that may vary from one company, region, or season to another.

WORK PROJECT

1. What are four ideas for building your professional wardrobe on a limited budget?
2. List four guidelines for selecting your corporate wardrobe.
3. What are four ideas for getting help with selection of a business wardrobe?

10

Coming and Going: Entering and Leaving the Corporate Nest

Anyone who says he isn't going to resign, four times, definitely will.

—John Kenneth Galbraith

"Look, I know your employee has been calling in sick quite a lot lately," one manager commented. "But that doesn't prove she's out looking for another job."

The other replied, "That's true. But how should I react when she calls in and says she's been called back for a second interview . . . with her doctor?"

You have been hired for a new job. During your first week in the unfamiliar environment, you are expected to offer an opinion in a meeting, mediate a conflict, and head up a complicated project. In the middle of all of that, you struggle to learn the rules of the corporate culture, remember the names of other people, and memorize the jargon and buzzwords unique to the company. And you're still not sure where the lunchroom is located.

Starting a new job is stressful for a number of reasons, the least of which is the need to learn to the work skills of your position. The rules of etiquette in the new organizational culture are likely to be far more complex to learn than the job requirements and are at least as critical to your survival in the job as the technical skills you possess.

A new set of rules also applies when you leave a company. In this chapter, we'll cover the rules of etiquette that apply when you start a new job and when you leave.

GUIDELINES FOR NEW EMPLOYEES

Starting out in a new job is frightening. Many of the unspoken rules that applied in your last position no longer apply. And regardless of what you have learned about the new company during the interview process, you may find that the actual environment is vastly different than you expected.

Example: You were recently hired to head up a twenty-five-person department. You discover several facts during the first week that they didn't tell you during the job interview. A serious rivalry exists between your department and the one situated next to it; the employees don't even speak to one another. Procedures are extremely disorganized, and work is perpetually three to four weeks behind. Morale in the department is extremely low.

You may discover an equal number of surprises even when you transfer from one department to another. The morale, political environment, and cultural rules may vary between floors. The differences may be so extreme that it's just like leaving one company and going to work for another.

Example: You were the manager of a corporate department, and you recently applied for an opening in one of the divisions. The offices are in the same building. You transfer from the sixth floor to the fifth. You are surprised to find that morale, attitude, and motivation among your new staff members are extremely positive. There were many problems in your previous job, and you expected to find the same situation in the new one.

Never assume that conditions in one department reflect the conditions throughout the company. Perspectives may be completely different, depending on the leadership, staffing, pressure from top management, contact with customers and vendors, and relationships with other departments and divisions.

When you first start your new job, follow the rules of etiquette and survival listed below and summarized in Figure 10-1:

1. *Keep a low profile.* Remember how people react when their environment is changed. Whether the change comes in the form of new procedures, a new manager or executive, automation, or new product lines, the tendency is to resist and fear the change—even if it represents an improvement over the past.

When you start your new job, don't assume that you are expected to make drastic changes, at least until you have been present for a while. The low profile will eventually reduce the apprehension others feel. As a new manager, *you* are the change and the perceived threat. That condition will fade away on its own as long as you start out slowly and demonstrate to everyone that you are not going to disrupt the work environment—at least not right away.

Figure 10-1. New managers: rules of etiquette.

1. Keep a low profile.

2. Consolidate your position slowly.

3. Ask a lot of questions.

4. Learn the unspoken rules.

5. Suggest improvements but proceed cautiously.

2. *Consolidate your position slowly.* You are expected to suggest changes and improvements, in time. However, you are also allowed a period of adjustment before you are expected to change radically the way things are done. Respect employee resistance to change, and let it run its course. In that way, you will build alliances rather than create more resistance.

When you do want to make changes, speak to those employees in the department who will be affected. Explain your reasons for wanting a change. Gear your arguments to improvement in *their* working conditions. Don't do anything that appears to be change for the sake of change. Some employees see any suggested change as an effort on your part to put your territorial mark on the department, no matter how much sense the change makes. Work with staff. Make it a team effort, and the staff will help you to consolidate your position.

3. *Ask a lot of questions.* New managers should never assume that they are expected to have all the answers. However, under the pressure of taking on a new job, some people convey the impression that they know how to "clean up the mess" left by someone else. Remember, there might not be a mess, or employees might not see existing conditions as a problem. Rather than suggesting or implementing answers, begin by asking a lot of questions. Avoid expressing conclusions for a while. Realize that, for the first one to two months on the job, you are learning both the procedures in the department and the culture itself.

4. *Learn the unspoken rules.* Every department contains a delicate balance of relationships. Managers are rarely absolute leaders but must adjust to a number of subordinate personalities. For example, some employees are very passive and need to be led through their routines; others want to be given responsibility and authority to execute their jobs with minimal supervision.

In some cases, one staff member may oversee the work of others, acting as an unofficial supervisor. A new manager who enters the picture and, unaware of these conditions, begins assuming an entirely new hierarchy can only create disruption and resistance. Hold off imposing any particular leadership style until you get to know the personalities and relationships within the department. Later, when you are comfortable with the way things are operating, you will be in a better position to make any needed changes.

5. *Suggest improvements, but proceed cautiously.* Approach all change with great tact. Even though you have the authority by title to change procedures, you also need to build a team. Involve your staff in all changes, emphasizing ideas to make their jobs easier, to improve efficiency and accuracy, and to overcome existing problems.

Take this approach: Explain the problem to the employees as you perceive it. Ask the employees how their jobs could be improved and how they would change them if given the chance. During your dialogue, the employees might come up with the idea you already have in mind; in that case, change will be easy, since it's the employees' own idea. Or a better idea could come from the meeting.

Avoid mandating any change without the employees' cooperation and agreement, if possible. If, however, you know a change is needed but the employees resist all the way, you will need to explain why you want to make the change. You may suggest, "Let's try it my way for a month and see if it works better. Meanwhile, if you have any other ideas, please talk to me about them."

Also keep an open mind to the idea that changes might not be needed. For example, you may come into a department that has already tried your idea in the past and found that, for various reasons, it didn't work. Or the previous manager may have put in a great deal of time and effort to create a well-run, organized, efficient department. In that case, there is no immediate need to change. If you recognize that things are working well and you're able to just leave them alone, your staff will respect you and appreciate the low-key, hands-off approach.

WHEN TO SPEAK OUT

The transition from "new kid on the block" to accepted member of the organizational family takes time. During that transition, the primary rule of behavior to observe is: Don't speak until you are absolutely certain about your position, or until you can back up what you say.

Example: You were hired three weeks ago and have not yet had time to learn the rules of behavior that apply in your new company. You realize this when, during a meeting with top management, you suggest hiring a consultant to study a problem and make recommendations. To you, the idea makes sense but as soon as you speak, you see that the statement was a mistake. The subject is changed quickly. After the meeting, another manager takes you aside and explains, "The president hates consultants. It might be smart to drop the idea and never mention it again."

A suggestion that seems logical, innocent, and well-motivated to you could harm your reputation. In this example, the president happened to dislike consultants—a fact you could not possibly have known unless you had been told. The same president may have a number of other quirks. So perhaps the best question you could ask in this situation is, "What else should I know before the next meeting?" As a strategy, set one important rule for yourself: Check with someone else before speaking out.

There are four reasons to speak out, either in front of subordinates or in meetings. They are:

1. *To find information on procedures or rules.* New managers are expected to ask many questions concerning procedures and company rules. You need to gather information in a relatively short period of time because—even though you are new—you will be expected to take over the reins of leaderships rather quickly.

Example: You have kept a low profile since being hired less than a month ago. You are relatively quiet at meetings and have not imposed sweeping changes in your department. However, you have also been observing carefully, making plans for changes you would like to implement in the near future. You have set specific goals: to improve efficiency, reduce expenses, and train several employees to provide job rotation coverage.

2. *To communicate in both directions.* Communication works only when you speak *and* listen well. As a new manager, you need to establish a communications link with employees, other managers, and the executives in your company. At first, the best rule of behavior is to communicate by listening carefully. Speak only to pose hypothetical solutions

and ask for feedback, to restate someone else's primary message to clarify it, or to lend verbal support to someone else's position.

> **Example:** On your third day in your new job, one of the employees in your department comes into your office to complain about another staff member. "We've been fighting for the last six months," the employee explains. Your strategy: After hearing the employee out, you call the other employee into your office to get the other side of the story. You then bring them in together. By asking a few questions, you create a dialogue between the two. The issues are not solved, but a compromise and temporary truce are reached. At the least, this defuses the conflict for the moment.

3. *To express ideas cautiously.* Just because you are new to the job does not mean you have to stay quiet. From the very first day, you should be able to express ideas, but you need to employ great tact at the same time.

> **Example:** You were hired to head a department that is highly disorganized. Work is late, the error rate is high, and employees are under constant pressure. You could make it clear that you are dissatisfied with the way things are being done and that you intend to improve conditions; however, that would only cause more disruption. Instead, you invite employees to bring problems to your attention; in each instance, you ask them how they would improve procedures. From this comes a number of recommendations, which you institute at once. In this case, change becomes acceptable, because it's achieved in cooperation with the staff.

4. *To solve employee problems.* You may be thrust into the middle of an ongoing conflict between employees or find yourself faced with a training problem. Your subordinates might fear or even resent your presence. In cases involving personalities, job skills, or conflict, you need to take a specific stand at once. You may not be able to resolve the problems quickly or easily, but you do need to prepare yourself to act as trainer, mediator, and counselor.

> **Example:** On your first day in the new job, one of the employees in the department comes to you and states that the company

should have promoted him to your job, rather than hiring someone from the outside. Your response: You place him in charge of a major project inherited from the previous manager. You give him complete authority for the project, with only one provision: He must keep you informed of progress. The employee excels and becomes a firm ally—in time.

In this example, two worthy goals were achieved. First, you defused the immediate problem by sharing authority and responsibility with the employee. Giving him an important task distracted him from his bitterness at being passed over for the management job. Second, the new assignment gave the employee valuable management experience. That experience can be tapped later. Rather than living with an enemy in the department, you created a lasting ally through your diplomatic action. You upgraded the quality of departmental resources, while also making your job easier.

Making positive and lasting change is a process, not an instant event. You may need to plant a seed and allow it to grow. As a rule of etiquette, recognize the fact that other people act and react for good reasons. You may need to work with or around those reasons in order to succeed as a newly-hired manager.

THE PROBATIONARY PERIOD

You should be aware of the probationary period whenever you are hired into a new job. The period usually lasts three months. The terms of your agreement might call for a performance review, salary adjustments, and qualifications for employee benefits at the end of the probationary term.

The conditions of the probationary period are spelled out specifically as part of the employment contract. There is another probationary period, however, that is rarely mentioned and never written down. That's the social and cultural probation. You will be judged by your performance as a member of the organizational family during this period. The unspoken questions on the minds of others will include:

- Do you deserve respect?
- Do you support and protect subordinates?
- Are you motivated to create alliances and work as part of a team, or are you only interested in serving your own interests?
- Are you honest or hypocritical?
- Do you have a volatile temper?
- Are you a demanding boss?
- Are you doing to drastically change and, thus, disrupt life in the department?

All these questions are on the minds of everyone in your department. Being aware of the social probationary period and the rules that limit what you can do and say and how you act during it will help you to survive it.

How do you know when the social probationary period is over? Unlike the official probation, no sudden changes or acknowledgements mark its end. It may take more time for some managers' social probation to end than for others, depending on personality, the difficulties encountered in the department, and how the manager copes with them.

The probation ends gradually, in small phases rather than in one sudden change. You will sense it is ending when others—notably subordinates—become relaxed around you, are comfortable speaking with you, and begin recommending change or improvement on their own. In other words, the programs you want to implement will not necessarily begin with your actions; instead, the people in your department will let you know, by accepting you, when the time is right and when the rules are changing.

The rules of etiquette will change when your social probation ends, again in gradual phases. You will be free to speak, even to implement changes in a more relaxed manner, without creating the perception that you are disrupting the status quo. However, all changes, even those made by seasoned managers who have been around for years, should be gently eased into the scene, rather than suddenly imposed in a communications vacuum. In meetings and dialogues, you need to employ tact in recommending change or even stating observations, no matter how long you have been with the company. Eventually, you cease to be the "new" manager; dissent, unpopular opinion, and complaints will become more acceptable once your colleagues know your name.

The etiquette may change in other ways after your probationary period:

1. *Others become familiar with your style.* Your style might represent a drastic departure from the style of the previous manager of the department. Other members of the company will need time to get used to you. Once they do, you will be accepted more readily. It is poor form to impose your ideas before you have been accepted by your staff.

2. *Your policies and priorities become known.* Each manager adopts a personal list of priorities. For some, the main goal is meeting budgets; for others, it is marketing. You may be very aware of your subordinates and take a personal interest in keeping them fulfilled and motivated, or you might prefer spending time in long-term planning meetings. Everyone has an individual style; people need time to discover yours.

3. *Your track record speaks for you.* Nothing speaks for you as well as success. You may tackle an especially difficult project and make a name for yourself quickly, or you might be the first manager of your department to meet deadlines every month or complete the year within budget. Once you prove your abilities, the etiquette will relax and others will come to depend on you. Of course, some will envy your performance and respond suspiciously, but most managers and executives will recognize your value, helping to end your probationary period.

LOOKING FOR A NEW JOB

Leaving a company has its own set of rules. The guidelines to follow vary, depending on whether you plan to tell your company you are looking for another job. If you do state your intentions, inform prospective employers of your availability. Let them know they may contact your current employer to confirm your position, dates of employment, and salary history. Also, don't misuse sick leave privileges. Arrange appointments before or after work hours or during your lunch hour, or take vacation time or days off without pay to attend interviews.

If you do not want to tell your current employer that you are looking for a new job, remember these rules:

1. *Ask prospective employers to not contact your current employer.* If you are currently working, most companies will ask you whether they may contact your current employer. If you ask them not to, chances are they will make that contact after you have accepted a new position to confirm what you report on your application and the statements you make in the interview.

2. *Arrange interviews on your own time.* It is poor form to use sick leave to go to job interviews. Take vacation time or leave without pay.

3. *Don't confide in anyone at work.* If you do not plan to tell your boss you are looking for a new job, you should keep your intentions to yourself, at least until you have accepted a new position and given notice. Don't confide in others at work; gossip has a way of being repeated. It is also unprofessional to give out the word that you're leaving. The exception, of course, is when you work with someone who is also a trusted and close friend.

A different set of rules applies when you plan to move from one division to another. If you will still be employed in the same company, observe these rules:

1. *Tell your current boss.* If you plan to apply for a different job in the same company, the first step should be to speak with your current supervisor. Let him or her know you are interested in the other position. This is not just a courtesy; it allows your boss time to think about finding a replacement if you are accepted in the new job.

Failing to advise your boss can create a very negative reaction, especially if the boss finds out only when news of approval reaches him or her. It appears disloyal and disrespectful for you to operate behind your supervisor's back, even if that wasn't your intention.

An exception to this rule: You needn't inform your boss if you are making the move primarily because the two of you are in conflict. In that case, informing the boss of your intentions might just cause trouble or even prevent your getting the other position.

2. *Make the application through proper channels.* Observe the proper application process in your company. If jobs are posted and applications invited, go through that route. Don't try to meet with the executive in charge of another division to get the inside track.

An exception: If you are aware of a pending opening and have a good relationship with the executive in the other division, you may speak to that person and express an interest in the job. However, once that is done, you should still follow the rules for posted jobs and submit your application properly.

3. *Suggest a transitional training period.* Help your current supervisor and your department by suggesting a temporary transitional period. Express your willingness to be available to the new manager to explain procedures, recurring deadlines, and other work-related issues. Also check with your supervisor in the new position to ensure that time will be allowed for a cooperative transition. One to two days over a two-week period should be enough; only a few hours of time are normally required to help a new manager. You demonstrate a willingness to help by suggesting the transition.

TURNING OVER WORK

When you are planning to leave—meaning you have already given notice but are still on the job—you should observe these rules:

1. *Don't complain about the company.* Your loyalty to your employer should continue right up to the moment you leave, even if you have legitimate complaints. It does no good to express your complaints to those who will still be working there. Chances are other employees are aware of any problems you have encountered. Use discretion in discussing anything about the company when you are in the outbound transition. If you want to express complaints, save them for your exit interview. If your company does not ask for your reasons for leaving, write a letter to the president after you leave and explain your concerns in detail.

2. *Continue to take your job seriously.* Show up to work on time, don't take excessive coffee breaks or lunch hours, and stay until quitting time. Continue performing the duties of the job as diligently as possible as long as you're still on the payroll. Remember, once you leave, people

will remember you by the way you performed your job, including your attitude and actions in the last two weeks.

3. *Let everyone know you're leaving.* Once you have given notice, there is no reason to keep your impending job change confidential. For a number of reasons, it is good behavior to let others know you are leaving. First, it is a social courtesy. Second, there may be pending projects, assignments, or ongoing job routines that need to be documented or explained before you leave. Make your transition an easy one for everyone else.

4. *Give positive reasons for your decision.* No matter how angry you are at your company's management, explain your reasons for leaving in a positive manner. For example, rather than saying, "This is a dead-end job," convey the same idea by explaining, "I took a position with greater career advancement potential."

If you have the opportunity to meet your replacement, your primary duty should be to ensure a smooth transition in which workflow is interrupted as little as possible. For example, if you have been promoted, a new manager may come in during your last two weeks in the old position. Work with that person. Spend time writing down procedures you've kept in your head. Help the new manager to master the job as quickly and as easily as possible.

You may continue to influence work in progress when you are promoted. For example, if you are offered a job in another division when you are halfway through an important project, you may be able to negotiate a longer transitional period to allow you to complete the project over the next two months or to share the project with the incoming manager, slowly phasing yourself out of the picture. Continuing to hold influence over work in progress may be one way to demonstrate that you are loyal to the company and that you take the job seriously. It is also a way to continue lending support to your department, even after you leave.

PREPARING FOR THE NEW MANAGER

It is common for an employee to leave without meeting his or her replacement. If that is the case for you, you can take a number of steps to help prepare for the change. These include:

1. *Document your key responsibilities.* Prepare step-by-step task descriptions for any work you know the new manager will have to take over. Be specific. Provide details about the report or task; list steps in order; tell where information comes from and where it goes; include the names of staff members and other managers involved in the task.

2. *Prepare flowcharts for recurring tasks.* Prepare simple flowcharts for all tasks you have performed yourself. Show not only the steps but also the sources of information: peoples' names, departments, and the type of information provided. Also provide supporting documents in the form of samples of past reports or filled-in forms.

3. *List special problem areas the new manager will need to know.* Prepare a priority list. Let the new manager know where the problems are in the department and what steps you have taken to deal with them.

4. *Instruct staff to document their tasks and to help the new manager.* Encourage your subordinates to organize their tasks with completed and updated job descriptions and task outlines. If you use a procedures manual, use your last weeks to update it for the new manager—for your job as well as the jobs of everyone in the department.

Although you may be leaving because you are dissatisfied with the company or with the job, maintain the decorum of a loyal company employee and do all you can to make the transition a smooth one. Make it a goal for yourself to be remembered as a professional, highly motivated, and loyal manager.

If you decide to stay on the job and work to solve any departmental problems rather than leave, you need to be aware of the rules for effective complaining. If you combine the skills of an outspoken manager and a polished diplomat, you can make a difference. Most managers need to express complaints at some point. The method you use often determines whether you have an influence and even whether others listen to you. The next chapter gives you ideas for complaining in a positive, progressive way.

WORK PROJECT

1. List and explain three rules of etiquette for newly-hired managers.
2. What are the four reasons to speak out when you have been on the job only a short time?
3. What are the three rules to observe when moving from one job to another in the same company?

11

Complaints: Speaking Out With Diplomacy

He that hath the worst cause makes the most noise.

—Thomas Fuller

"The people in my department are constantly complaining," the manager said to the executive. "I find myself making lame excuses just to get away from them. How do you suggest I handle this situation?"

"I'd love to discuss this," the executive answered, hurriedly rising from his chair. "But I've got to run. I think I hear my mom calling."

Your department is overworked and understaffed. That budget they forced on you won't ever cover the first half of the year. Your boss is intolerable, demanding, and unresponsive. You had a great idea and presented it at the last staff meeting, but no one would listen. And yesterday, your dog died.

If you find that your complaints are not listened to or handled in a satisfactory manner, it may mean you need a new approach. Whether you have a number of unresolved issues or others come to you with their problems and you don't know how to respond, you can improve the situation by developing your own guidelines. The rules of effective complaint management could simplify your professional life.

THE NEGATIVE APPROACH

Some people get into the habit of communicating their problems to someone else, expecting the other person to come up with a solution. They burn their bridges. They overlook what should be obvious: When you burn a bridge on one side, it becomes useless on the other side as well.

Taking a negative approach may be your first impulse, but it's an impulse worth resisting. Before expressing any idea to someone else, stop and think. How will it sound to the other person? Is the issue that person's problem, or is it yours? Would a team effort be the best approach to arriving at a solution? The rule of etiquette when you communicate a complaint to someone else is: Take responsibility for the solution, even if only as one of several participants. Try to avoid the assumption that your job is to bring a problem to someone else's attention and that the other person's job is to fix it.

When you take the negative approach, you also gain the reputation you most want to avoid. You become known as a complainer, rather than as an action–oriented problem solver. This attribute does not inspire others to work with you cooperatively, but forces them away.

Example: One manager fell into the habit of complaining bitterly to his boss, co-workers, and anyone else who would listen. Solutions rarely came from this process, but he didn't see that the problem was in his approach. On those occasions when the manager did have a constructive recommendation to offer, no one would listen. They were accustomed to his negative style.

Managers who are perceived as complainers do not have a voice in the management process. They lose the respect of their subordinates, other managers, and top management. They become ineffective. They have not learned the rule of behavior that would allow them to join the team—that problem solvers get things done, while those who merely complain are isolated, left out of the loop.

Listen to your style of communication. Avoid negative statements. Come up with more positive ways to state your concerns. For example, consider these negative statements and the positive alternatives:

Negative	*Positive*
I hate it when . . .	Wouldn't it be better if . . .
Why can't you . . .	What if we . . .
This is stupid . . .	What about this alternative . . .
This will never work out because . . .	I had another idea you might consider . . .

Expressing yourself in negative terms creates the impression in others that you see issues only in the most negative way. That does not lead to cooperation; it only causes other people to avoid working with you.

People also feel alienated from those who express themselves in absolute terms. If you find yourself falling into this habit, fight the impulse. It comes from wanting to emphasize your position but often produces an outcome that is the opposite of what you wish to achieve. For example, consider the following absolute statements and the alternatives:

Absolute	*Nonabsolute*
He always says . . .	I have heard him say . . .
Nothing ever gets done around here . . .	We have had problems at times . . .
Everyone thinks . . .	Many people seem to think . . .
We must do it this way . . .	Here's a good idea to consider . . .

When you communicate in positive and nonabsolute terms, you receive the response you seek. Those who employ the diplomatic approach may complain just as much as others, but with this difference—people listen to them and are more likely to respond. For example, think about the people with whom you work—your staff, other managers, and executives. You are probably more willing to respond when they communicate with you in positive, motivating terms. Those who come to you only with complaints that they expect you to solve elicit resistance or unwilling compliance.

THE POSITIVE APPROACH

When you see an issue from two points of view, you have twice the information. The ability to understand the other person's priorities and concerns makes you a more effective participant in the discussion; having only your own opinion complicates the task.

You learn about the other point of view by listening carefully. If you hear the message but don't know why the other person takes a particular position, ask questions. Get information. You might change your mind, or at least broaden your comprehension, by seeing the issue from another perspective.

Example: The monthly report you prepare has been held up for each of the last three months because another department didn't get information to you in time. Your first impulse is to register a complaint with that department's manager and to demand that the information be delivered on time in the future, without exception. However, instead of creating a confrontation, you meet with the manager, raise the issue, and then listen. You discover that the problem is not in that department, but somewhere else. The information has been late because the department did not receive what it needed on time. As the result of this dialogue, you and the other manager now can work together to solve the problem.

In this example, you may need to ask for a later deadline, track down the source of the problem and ask for a quicker response, or develop the information from a different source. The point is, by finding out why a problem came up, rather than making demands or registering your complaint, the real problem is identified and the probable solution is made clearer.

Before complaining, find out what elements are involved in the problem. Consider the entire issue, not just one or two aspects of it. Your department is part of a larger machinery, comparable to a person in a fire brigade who must quickly pass buckets of water from one person to another and who complains to the chief that the people closer to the well are not passing buckets quickly enough. The real problem might be that it takes a long time to lower and raise the bucket because the well is so deep. The chief will resist responding to a complaint about the line when he's aware of the problem with the well. It would be more constructive to suggest dropping stones into the well, to raise the water level.

When you comprehend the larger problem and need to register a complaint, also consider the issue of profit. You will receive a better response by offering solutions that improve profits, rather than demanding a solution from someone else.

> **Example:** Your staff of fourteen people operates with only three computer terminals. You need six. You approach your boss with this problem and ask for approval to purchase three additional terminals.
>
> *Alternative 1:* You complain that three other departments with fewer employees have more terminals than you do. The statement you offer: "You let them buy more terminals; why can't I?"
>
> *Alternative 2:* You prepare a summary of idle time—employees waiting for a terminal to become free. Based on average hourly pay, you estimate the cost of idle time to the company. Your study shows that the cost of three additional terminals will be recaptured within less than six months. From that point forward, the investment will become profitable. Approval of your idea makes sense.

The first idea—comparing one department to another—is negative. It places responsibility for a solution somewhere else, delegating the problem away from the department. The second idea is more constructive. It registers the complaint, but only in the context of a specific and profitable solution.

You are probably aware that many people complain using the first alternative. Employees in your department may look to you to solve their problems, although, in many instances, they would do better to come to you with recommendations rather than merely complaining. The same idea applies when you take a complaint to someone else.

The steps to take in developing the positive approach to complaining are:

- Educate yourself. Understand the other person's point of view and how he or she sees the problem. Ask questions and create a dialogue.
- Look at the problem from the broadest possible perspective. Recognize that your department sees only a small part of the whole picture.
- Don't just complain; come up with one or more possible solutions. Look for opportunities to recommend change that also improves profits.

These steps, taken together, become a procedure you can use to complain effectively. They also conform to this rule of behavior: You have a responsibility to comprehend problems from the other person's point of view, thus respecting their concerns. Your ability to do so is enhanced when you see issues from the organizational point of view rather than the departmental. And you are most likely to elicit a positive response from others when you propose a solution that is also profitable.

HANDLING COMPLAINTS FROM OTHERS

There are two sides to the etiquette of effective complaining—you may need to complain to your supervisor, to other managers, or even to subordinates, and others may come to you with their own complaints. Creating a positive approach in others requires good communication skill and diplomacy. You need to train people in the art of positive, constructive complaining. You can achieve this by responding to the positive approach and by showing by example how a negative message can be turned into a positive one. Employ these techniques when someone comes to you with a complaint:

1. *Make sure you understand the message.* You may hear one complaint when, in fact, a different one is intended. You clarify by asking questions at the right moment.

Example: An employee in your department who spends several hours per day working on a computer terminal comes into your office and complains that her job is too difficult. The system is slow to respond, the workload is too large, and no one knows how difficult it is to sit there for hours. You restate the complaint: "So you're saying that the job is difficult?" The employee answers, "No, I'm saying I'm bored."

2. *Offer hypothetical solutions.* Encourage others to think in positive terms by suggesting possible solutions to them. This is preferable to imposing a solution or accepting the delegated problem.

Example: The manager of another department meets with you and complains that your employees work too slowly. The result: His department cannot meet its month-end deadlines. You suggest: "Would the situation improve if you and I met half-way through the month and did a review?"

3. *Listen more than you speak.* Give other people the time to make their case. Listen carefully to what they say; observe their body language and tone; pay close attention. Some people come to you to verbalize a complaint and, in the process of speaking, arrive at solutions all on their own.

Example: An employee brings a problem to you. A task involves filling out a six-part form several times per day, although, in most cases, only four parts are needed. The employee complains about the inefficiency, cost, and red tape involved. Then a solution occurs to the employee: "Maybe we should order a four-part form next time we run out. Then, when we do need extra parts, we could photocopy them."

4. *Ask for a solution.* When someone comes to you and registers a complaint, your first inclination might be to propose a solution, to accept the complaint as your problem. However, you may also consider asking the person for ideas. This not only forces the other person to think; it also conveys the idea that you respect the person's opinion.

Example: An employee in your department complains that it's taking too much time to complete a particular task each day. You hear him out and then ask, "How would you suggest we change procedures?" Another possible response: "I'd like you to think about a more efficient way this can be done. Write it up and bring it to me."

RULES OF RESPONSE

When other people bring complaints to you, be aware that your reaction will either lead to a solution or freeze the problem. This rule of behavior should be observed: Trying to make problems go away is not a solution; you owe it to others to work for a solution.

A dialogue can become a confrontation when one side does not understand this essential point. If you find yourself in the middle of a confrontation, use these techniques to achieve a positive result:

1. *Stick to the issues.* Don't let confrontations dissolve into unrelated accusations. Keep the issue in mind. A confrontation should never become personal and should be directed toward solution rather than ongoing debate without resolution.

Example: Two people are arguing, and it become obvious that each is sticking to her position. One becomes frustrated and states, "It's impossible to talk to you. You're just too close-minded."

2. *Refuse to argue.* You might be absolutely right in your position, but the other person may want only to argue with you. Don't allow yourself to be pulled into an argument that won't lead to a solution.

Example: An employee is chronically late to work. When you warn him to be on time, he complains, "You're always picking on me." Your first impulse is to answer, "That's because you're the only one who always comes in late." That statement will lead to denial, even to the employee's presenting examples of other employees being late. The argument can be defused by not responding in this way. Here's an illustration of how this can be done:

> Employee: You're always picking on me.
> Manager: Regardless, I expect you to get to work on time.
> Employee: But that's not fair!
> Manager: Even so, I expect you to follow the rules.
> Employee: They're too strict, and I don't like them.
> Manager: I understand. But that's the way it is. The rules stand.

Notice that the manager does not respond to the arguments made by the employee: It's not fair, you're picking on me, the rules are too strict. Every response goes back to the issue. After two or three of these exchanges, the wind goes out of the complainer's sail, because you refuse to respond in an argumentative way.

3. *Use "I" messages.* Avoid threatening people by placing blame on them. Express your thoughts with "I" messages. Compare these examples concerning a problem of chronic tardiness to see how the same message can be made less intimidating and, often, clearer:

Example of a "You" message: You tell the employee, "You can't come in late. That's not acceptable. If you're late again, you're going to be in big trouble."

Example of an "I" message: You express the same idea from a different point of view: "I enforce these rules for a good reason, and I expect everyone to respect them. I want you here on time."

4. *Propose compromise.* Confrontations lead to impasse. If the confrontation is not managed well, a solution will be impossible. In fact, even the easiest problems, those with obvious solutions, may escalate and become complicated when both sides refuse to give in. The solution is to propose compromises. Some people just don't know how to work with you, and you may need to get along with them by entering a series of treaties.

Example: Your department prepares information that is sent to another department, usually by the 20th of the month. The manager of the other department asks you to complete this work by the 10th; that would give you only three days, and you need at least six. You propose a compromise: The work will be delivered no later than the 16th.

Rules of behavior in the organizational culture may call for diplomacy. Three skills are worth developing: apologizing, educating, and tolerating.

You may find that, even when your position is right, it is sometimes more constructive to apologize than to stick stubbornly to one point of view. In many instances, an apology is a diplomatic strategy rather than an acceptance of responsibility. The apology can also defuse the complaint, especially when you are unable to solve it.

Example: The manager of another department has come to you to complain about information sent from your department. He needs more than what you supply. The expanded data the manager wants are not available to you. Your response: "I'm sorry that the report we give you isn't complete. But we simply don't have what you need."

You may also use the second technique—educating the other person, in this case by explaining why the information is not available to you. The complaint may be legitimate but misdirected. You will probably have opportunities to educate employees in two ways—by helping them to master the art of complaining constructively and by training them to recognize how to direct complaints to the right person or department.

Example: One of your employees works closely with the staff of another department. Your employee complains to you, "The manager is very hostile toward me for no good reason. I don't want to go over there any more." You could try to intercede and solve the problem, which may be what your employee wants. However, it might be more valuable to offer other ideas, such as: "Have you thought about inviting the manager to lunch and working out the problem away from the pressure of the office?"

You can also educate employees by expanding their point of view. For example, an employee complains that top management imposes new tasks and that "they don't even know what's going on." Your response may be to bring to the employee's attention a number of factors of concern at the top: the competition, stockholders, the need to expand product lines, cash flow restrictions. Any number of management priorities are beyond the vision of an employee involved in meeting daily pressures for a narrowly focused series of tasks.

The third skill is tolerance. As a manager, you are sometimes expected to just listen and not solve problems for subordinates. You are not compelled always to offer advice. Some people just need to express their problems to you. Look for signs that someone only needs you to listen, such as expressions like, "I know this is my problem, but. . . ." In these cases, don't assume that you're expected to come up with answers.

> **Example:** An employee comes into your office and exclaims, "I'm really upset!" You ask what's going on and realize it's a personality conflict between the employee and someone in another department. After five minutes of letting off steam, the employee leaves.

In this case, you provided a valuable service. You were available to someone who needed to vent steam; no solution was asked for or expected. Even though this service is not part of their job description, many managers end up spending a good part of their day acting as a sounding board, surrogate parent, social worker, or sympathetic friend.

PROTECTING YOUR BOSS

You expect subordinates to respect you and to demonstrate loyalty to you and to the department. You would not tolerate an employee going over your head with work, recommendations, or complaints. You owe the same respect to your boss.

One situation you may encounter is hearing a complaint from someone else about your boss. For example, a fellow manager who reports to the same vice-president may come to you and state, "He's a real idiot. I hate working for him." How do you deal with this situation without offering the sympathy and support the other person might expect? Some guidelines:

1. *Ask for more information.* Ask the other person what happened that led him or her to make the statement. You will probably hear the details of an incident and may then respond with an idea, such as, "That was insensitive, but you should speak to him if you expect the problem to go away."

2. *Offer a professional solution.* Once you know why the other person is complaining, suggest direct contact with the source: "Why don't you meet with the vice-president and explain your position? Offer a compromise so it doesn't happen again."

3. *State your loyalty.* Be sure you explain that you respect the chain of command. You should not take part in gossip or complaints as long as they're not constructive. You may even go on to say, "If that happened to me, I'd probably want to meet with him and lay it out on the table."

If you run into conflict with your boss and are unable to solve it directly, you may have to reinforce your position at the departmental level or go even higher in the chain of command.

Example: The vice-president has been approaching employees in your department directly and giving out assignments. You meet with the vice-president and explain, "It creates conflict in the department. I give them an assignment and then you contradict it. If you would come to me first, I could delegate the work for you. I want the employees to have to report to only one person."

Example: You report to a senior manager who has been making inappropriate advances to one of the female employees in your department. She has reported the incidents to you, and, in response, you approached the senior manager and asked him to stop. But the problem continues. After this occurs twice, you document the problem and go above his head.

Two rules to observe:

1. *The chain of command should be broken only in extreme cases.* You should work through your immediate supervisor in nearly all cases; the

only exceptions are extreme situations such as sexual harassment, illegal acts, or theft of company property. If a problem cannot be solved by going to the source, you have a loyalty that surpasses your loyalty to the chain of command—loyalty to your subordinates and to the company.

2. *Always document the situation.* A suspicion of wrongdoing is not enough. If you plan to bring a problem to the attention of a higher power, first gather your facts, document them, and be prepared to prove your case. For example, a complaint of sexual harassment should include a written statement from the victim. If your supervisor instructs you to falsify information or otherwise break the law, write down the details of the conversation before formally making your complaint. If you know your boss is embezzling, write down your proof. Don't break the chain of command with only a suspicion or with hearsay. If you can't prove your case, *your* career and reputation will be on the line.

GUIDELINES FOR REGISTERING COMPLAINTS

By establishing rules of behavior for handling either side of a complaint, you will make your job easier and will be able to overcome the common problems: unwanted confrontations, unresolved problems, and polarized points of view. Guidelines are summarized below and in Figure 11-1:

1. *Plan your message.* When delivering a complaint to someone else, first decide what you want to express. If it helps, draw up a list of your major points. A few moments invested in organizing your thoughts will make the difference between a time-wasting exercise and a constructive, helpful dialogue.

2. *Offer a solution.* Make it a personal standard never to complain without having at least one solution ready. Emphasize profits when complaining to decision makers, rather than expecting someone else to solve your problem for you.

3. *Concentrate on the positive.* Express yourself clearly but in the most positive way possible. Avoid negative statements and absolutes; use "I" messages to avoid threats or accusations. When someone complains to you, employ communication techniques to improve your response: listen

Figure 11-1. Guidelines: rules for complaining.

1. Plan your message.

2. Offer a solution.

3. Concentrate on the positive.

4. Manage confrontation.

5. Explore alternatives.

6. Examine all sides of the issue.

carefully, clarify what you believe the person is saying, pose hypothetical solutions, and ask the other person to offer a solution to you.

4. *Manage confrontation.* Don't allow others to draw you into an argument, to stray from the real issues, or to force you into a position from which the dispute cannot be resolved.

5. *Explore alternatives.* Any problem may have an infinite number of possible solutions. You may believe you can identify the best one, but also keep an open mind. Your job is far easier when you lead others to solutions than when you must come up with the answers on your own. Always look for better ideas from someone else, and be prepared to abandon the position you previously held.

6. *Examine all sides of the issue.* Be aware of the broadest possible range of the problem. The viewpoint from your department might allow you to see a very small part of a larger issue. Also remain sensitive to the priorities in other departments and of the pressures under which subordinates operate.

You can become an effective, outspoken complainer in your company without damaging your reputation. Work on discovering effective methods for conveying your ideas and suggesting solutions to problems. You will find that complaining in a positive manner is a worthwhile career skill.

WORK PROJECT

1. Express the following negative statements in positive form:
   a. No one understands what I have to put up with.
   b. Why do I always get the big problems?
   c. Why can't you take care of this without bothering me?
   d. This isn't my problem.
2. List profit-oriented ways to communicate the following problems:
   a. You need more floor space for your crowded department.
   b. Your photocopy machine breaks down frequently.
   c. You are forced to spend too much time ordering supplies for your department.
3. What are the three steps to take in developing a positive approach to complaining?

12

Use of Time: Scheduling Your Career

Since the early bird catches the worm, it's a good idea to begin your day as soon as you can—unless, of course, you happen to be a worm.

—Edwin C. Bliss

"I'm having problems explaining the concept of time management to one of my employees," Betty said to Susan. "I told him to pretend he was a cab driver, constantly watching the meter."

"That sounds like a good idea," Susan replied. "What went wrong?"

"Now he takes a longer route to work. He's been late every day this week."

So much of what defines professional attitude has to do with management of time. Do you arrive promptly for meetings? Do you control your telephone? Do you set a good example for subordinates? The way you answer these questions determines your awareness of time etiquette.

The way you manage time shows your awareness of the rules of behavior. It sets a tone for your organizational style and shows others that you respect the value of their time—or that you do not.

THE PROMPTNESS ETHIC

The company expects employees to arrive at work on time, to take no more than the specified time allowed for breaks and for lunch, and to stay at work until quitting time. These rules are specified in the employee handbook. However, within the day, promptness rules may be more relaxed and informal. People may show up late for meetings or miss appointments. Such behavior may be so common that it becomes normal and acceptable.

A worthwhile rule of behavior to set for yourself is: Show courtesy and respect to others by being on time for meetings and by keeping appointments.

Should you be precisely on time for an appointment? Or is it better to arrive early or late? A lot of significance—perhaps too much—has been placed on the statement you make by when you arrive. The generalization claims that if you show up early, it's a sign that you are subservient to the other person, and perhaps too anxious; if you're late, you have the power advantage; and if you're right on time, you're too organized or too unflexible. (See Chapter 5 on appointments.) All of these ideas become custom, but living by the presumed rule takes something away from the professional attitude you want to convey. When an appointment is made for a specific time, it should be kept by both sides out of mutual courtesy. Forget the subtle messages implied by being early or late, and set a new rule for yourself: You will arrive on time whenever possible and will not allow yourself to fall into the customary trap of needing to make a silent statement.

The on-time ethic makes a favorable impression on others. You will be seen as having a responsible and professional attitude about honoring a promise. Some people may think you're too inflexible because you're always there at exactly the promised moment; don't allow that to change your rule.

It is better to be early than late. Showing up early may be inconvenient to someone else, in which case you should be willing to wait a few moments until the person is ready to meet with you. It's having to wait that leads to the belief that you will be at a disadvantage; the argument is that this places you in a secondary position and perhaps starts the meeting out poorly.

If you show up late, others are more likely to be irritated with you than to assume that you are the more powerful participant. Like many unspoken assumptions, this one is flawed. No one wants to be kept waiting because someone else wants to be fashionably late. That creates the impression that you're disorganized or that you don't respect the other person's schedule enough to be on time.

The manner in which you keep appointments not only sends a message to other managers and executives; it also tells subordinates a lot about you. If you set an example by being on time for appointments, your staff will tend to follow that example. If you're consistently late, you create the opposite role model. You have a high profile and provide a management example for your department to emulate, for better or worse.

Follow these guidelines to train employees to respect the promptness ethic:

1. *Be prompt yourself.* You send the clearest message to employees in the way you keep appointments with them. If you have scheduled an appointment with someone in your department, be on time. If you are prompt whenever you have appointments outside the department but apply a different standard when dealing with subordinates, the wrong message will be sent.

Example: The manager of a sales department set a standard: Never be late for appointments with the customer. However, when the manager had a meeting with a salesperson, he was chronically late. This sent a mixed message: "I expect you to be on time for your meetings, but I am unable to live by the rule myself."

2. *Expect promptness from staff, and say so.* It's not enough to develop an expectation regarding promptness; you also need to communicate it to staff. If you want your employees to be prompt, tell them. Make your position clear, and base it on the idea of respecting the value of other people's time. Set a policy you are able to live with, and expect your subordinates to follow suit.

Example: One manager had problems getting staff members to show up on time for appointments and meetings. But once she began expressing her standard, the problem was not as severe. She realized that all it took was for her to make her position clear to others.

3. *Train employees to set immediate goals tied to the clock.* Whether employees are attending a meeting or working to finish a task, show them how to perform as professionals, using the clock. Use time as a goal-setting device; having a deadline makes it easier to accomplish the desired result and, at the same time, forces people to follow the rule of courtesy.

Example: The department's work revolved around immediate deadlines. The manager showed employees how to plan completion time, which seemed to help people improve both their working style and organizational skills.

4. *Don't vary your standard based on rank.* Apply your standards equally, whether your appointment is with a subordinate, a fellow manager, or the president of the company. Respect for the importance of someone else's time extends across all ranks. Managers who show equal respect for the filing clerk and for the top executive gain the respect of subordinates.

Example: One manager was consistently on time for meetings with executives and fellow managers. But he often showed up late for appointments in his own department or failed to show up at all. The message: Subordinate time was not as important as management time.

MEETING AND TELEPHONE ETIQUETTE

You have the greatest opportunity to demonstrate your awareness of time etiquette in two common situations: when attending meetings and in using your telephone. Chapters 6 and 7 discussed the various rules of etiquette for meetings and telephone use; for the purpose of time management, a brief review is worthwhile.

Some guidelines for the time etiquette of meetings:

1. *Be on time—at the beginning and at the end of the meeting.* Whether you're an attendee or the leader of a meeting, show up on time and—whenever possible—leave when the meeting is over. If a stop time is not indicated, ask for one. Diplomatically teach others to place finite limits on their meetings.

It won't always be possible to leave a meeting on time, because agendas tend to run over. One technique you can use to force compliance with a promised time limit without offending others is to set up an appointment after the meeting. When the time arrives, excuse yourself and explain, "I have another appointment."

2. *Stick to the agenda.* As a meeting leader, organize your agenda so that all business can be covered in the time you have allowed. As an attendee, stick to the topics, and don't introduce unrelated ideas or begin discussions about business not on the agenda.

3. *Leave the disintegrated meeting.* A number of meetings approach an end and then meander, not quite finishing up. The attendees relax and keep discussions going, pause by the door and add fifteen minutes onto the time, or begin smaller side meetings. In a more extreme example, the meeting may fall apart altogether, with only a few agenda items being covered. Some organizations have meetings that quickly become crisis centers; the agenda is tossed aside because one or more attendees brings up unexpected business that has to be discussed at once.

When this occurs, you should leave. You have other priorities that day and should be visible back in your own department. You can end the disintegrated meeting firmly but courteously, sending the message that you will attend—but only as long as constructive discussions continue or as long as agenda topics are on the table. The crisis subject rarely is of concern to everyone at the meeting, and it is poor form to expect a number of people to waste time while that subject is being discussed; you don't necessarily have to take part.

The telephone is a convenience, but it can also subvert your good intentions. The way you control the phone or allow it to control you establishes your reputation. Because a ringing telephone is loud and distracting, the incoming call may be given the highest priority, no matter what else you're doing. And that's the problem. Guidelines for telephone time etiquette:

1. *Take control.* Don't allow the telephone to control you. Show that you respect the people you're meeting with now more than the incoming call and that you can create time away from the phone to complete priority tasks.

2. *Don't allow incoming calls to interrupt appointments.* Don't expect people to wait for you while you take an incoming call. You create a poor impression when you force someone to sit in your office because an unexpected call comes in. Have calls intercepted by someone else, or, if you must answer the phone, say you're in a meeting and promise to call back as soon as possible.

3. *Don't take calls in meetings or make calls into meetings.* Meetings should not be interrupted in person or by the phone. However, having a phone in the conference room makes interruption very easy. Never make calls into a meeting unless you have an emergency, and don't accept calls when you're in meetings yourself.

THE DISORGANIZED EXECUTIVE

You may be the most courteous, aware manager imaginable when it comes to the etiquette of time management in your own department. But what if you work for an executive who is not as aware? Some people never even see the impression created by discourteous time practices. In those cases, you may need diplomatically to train your boss in the rules of etiquette. Some ideas:

1. *Communicate in terms of time constraints.* When you meet with the disorganized executive, begin by explaining a time constraint. For example, you get together at 10 A.M. Begin by saying, "I have to be back by 11 for another appointment." This tells the executive there is a time constraint and leads to a better organized appointment.

Use the same technique when you depend on the executive to give you information. For example, your boss has given you an assignment to write a report; however, some of the information you need has to come from the boss. You may say, "I will be able to meet the deadline if I get this information by Tuesday."

2. *Check again before your deadline.* Receiving clear communications helps to train the executive to be more organized. However, that doesn't mean the technique will always work. You should plan to remind the executive of your time constraints. Before a scheduled appointment, call and ask, "Are we still on for 10 tomorrow?" Or, if you are waiting for information due by Tuesday, call and ask, "Can I come by and pick up those numbers this afternoon?"

3. *Organize for the executive.* Although you can train an executive to exercise more respect for your own time, you cannot always be as direct as you would be with a subordinate. You need to use greater diplomacy. One method is to organize for the executive; by setting an example, you prove that it's possible to organize better and at the same time solve a problem for the other person by removing the pressure and distraction and presenting workable solutions instead of making demands.

ETIQUETTE AND YOUR CAREER

You need to be aware of many rules, both spoken and unspoken, in your corporate culture. To the new employee, the rules are intimidating and complex; even the seasoned employee must constantly learn on the job. The way you use your time and teach others to use theirs sets the tone of your behavior.

To be perceived as a professional, responsible, and courteous manager requires adopting the right attitude and then putting it into practice. When you show that you respect other people's time, you gain a positive reputation. All forms of etiquette add to this favorable view; however, use of time is one of the most visible forms of organizational behavior.

When you practice responsible time management—by being prompt, keeping appointments, and applying sensible rules in meetings and for the control of the phone—you teach others by example. That is a trait of a leader, whether or not you hold a leadership title. When you are aware of the rules, you become a career survivor; anyone who fails to learn the rules limits his or her own potential.

It might be a healthier and simpler environment if all of the unspoken rules could be written down. However, the rules often change from one company or region to another or are altered with time. An expanding company changes the internal environment in every way; the unspoken rules in effect this month might be inapplicable in the next quarter. Similarly, whenver the size of a staff changes, the rules of etiquette may change as well. A small, friendly staff operating under very relaxed rules might become a highly structured department when a few more people are added. Each new employee brings along a series of personal goals and priorities, which further adds to change.

Even though etiquette is primarily involved with nonverbal customs and rules, it usually is based on common sense. Some organizations develop rules as part of a tradition that doesn't apply in any other company. But new employees quickly learn those rules and survive within their limits. The most essential rule of etiquette to follow is this: Observe and listen, think about how your messages are heard, and set a positive example for others.

WORK PROJECT

1. Explain why showing up for appointments on time makes the best impression.
2. List and discuss the four guidelines for training employees to follow the promptness ethic.
3. What are three ideas you can put into practice when you work with a disorganized executive?

Appendix
Work Project Answers

CHAPTER 1

1. The three popular myths about corporate custom are:
   a. *The first myth:* Popularity isn't important as long as you do your job well. The reality is that being popular with fellow employees is extremely important. Popularity also affects your future with the organization.
   b. *The second myth:* Each person's role is clearly defined by rank and title. The reality: Many employees have influence but do not hold rank or title. An unspoken rule is that you should understand the significance of the influence structure as well as the stated chain of command; you need to operate with that second organizational chart in mind.
   c. *The third myth:* The rules of behavior are nothing more than common sense. The reality: Although common sense does define most rules of behavior, many customs contradict this idea. You may need to accept and live with rules that make absolutely no sense.
2. Several rules define company loyalty, including:
   a. *Evaluate situations with the company's goals in mind.* This helps make difficult decisions and avoid personal biases.
   b. *Avoid taking part in gossip and rumor.* The true leader handles this problem consistently and fairly. He or she takes steps to discourage others from taking part in gossip and rumor; when a rumor is circulating, the leader tries to convince management to share information with employees.

    c. *Respect the chain of command.* Protect your supervisor by not going over or around to report, get information, or make decisions.

    d. *Communicate with everyone who is affected by your decisions.* This courtesy will avoid many problems and should be practiced even when you are not required to exercise it.

    e. *Think before you speak, then decide whether the timing is right.* Be aware that the message is not the entire issue; it often comes down to when and where it is conveyed.

    f. *Be aware that there are at least three agendas in every meeting.* The written agenda limits the topics of discussion; you have an agenda of your own; and every other person in the meeting has an individual agenda. The topics you raise and points you make should be approached with all of the agendas in mind.

3. Confrontations can best be managed by following these rules of behavior:

    a. *Get your facts.* Before you confront someone else, be sure you have information straight; if someone else confronts you, be sure you have the right information before responding.

    b. *Apologize if you are wrong.* Never try to get through a confrontation when you are not in the right; end the debate by apology.

    c. *In some cases, apologize even when you're right.* It may be that you cannot win with some people; ending the discussion may be more constructive than proving a point.

    d. *Respect subordinates in a confrontation.* If someone apologizes when he or she wasn't wrong, explain that there is no need to do so.

    e. *Always confront issues and not people.* Remember the principle of fair fighting, and stick to the issues.

CHAPTER 2

1. A political situation may grow in any number of ways, usually involving a combination of events and circumstances. Some of the more common of these are:

    a. *Human nature.* You need to find ways to work around people who won't cooperate otherwise. Trust is not automatic for everyone, so you may need to emphasize a positive approach and prove that you can be trusted.

b. *Communication from the top.* The leaders of your company may not always succeed in their job. It might become necessary for you and other middle managers to fill the void left when top management communicates poorly.

c. *Financial pressure.* Communication also fails when company leaders believe they must protect themselves and the organization. In that situation, the lack of facts allows the rumor mill to become active. Convey a message to the top: People will fill in the gaps if they are not given information. No matter how bad the news, truth is preferable to rumor.

d. *Changes at the top.* When new leadership arrives on the scene, it invariably disrupts the entire organization. You contribute a lot to making change a positive experience and set a positive example for your subordinates by offering your assistance to new leaders.

e. *Individual disruption.* Any person can bring a lot of problems to the corporate family. There may be little you can do to change others; however, you can improve the situation somewhat by not allowing your subordinates to take part in the conflict and by verbalizing the problem to the individual causing the disruption.

2. Power struggles, which so often characterize corporate life, are especially difficult to contend with. However, there are solutions:

a. *Individual rivalries.* Make an effort to establish rapport and trust with the other person. Do all you can to defuse the sense of mistrust.

b. *Departmental or divisional rivalry.* The problems that develop between areas of responsibility usually involve conflicts of work priority. For example, a marketing department and an administrative or service department probably see the same issues from a different point of view. The proper way to solve this problem is to seek common ground, remain flexible as to procedure, and resolve the problem through mutual agreement, compromise, or even truce.

c. *High profile in meetings.* Many people see the meeting as a stage, a place to gain a name with top management. You may have to tolerate this and proceed with caution, recognizing that some people may not deal with you honestly in all cases; once they get into a meeting, they might turn on you.

    d. *Priority of work and budgets.* No matter how much of a budget increase someone else is given, keep your focus on company profits and departmental performance. Don't let yourself be drawn into the competitive game.

3. Guidelines for neutralizing politics include:

    a. *Communicate directly with others.* Don't allow yourself to fall into the common trap of telling everyone but the source of the problem how you feel.

    b. *Don't play the influence game.* Concentrate on the tasks and goals of the department and not on the appearance of influence.

    c. *Don't worry about what others think or do.* Pay attention to business, and don't concern yourself with the immediate political victories others may win.

    d. *Provide a positive leadership role model.* The employees in your department watch you constantly. If you are a focused, strong leader, you will gain their loyalty and trust.

    e. *Present ideas from a position of strength.* Avoid placing yourself in situations in which you offer ideas but cannot back them up with facts or in which you have to defend a weak position.

    f. *Discuss new ideas with those affected by them.* Before presenting recommendations to management, first speak to other managers; find out their ideas, and incorporate their concerns in your proposal. This not only helps you avoid making enemies; it also increases trust between you and others.

CHAPTER 3

1. The rules vary from one company to another and may also change from rank to rank. Possible rules to be aware of include:

    a. *Use last names for executives.* This is a safe approach, to be used until you are given permission to use an informal style.

    b. *Use last names until told otherwise.* Here again, the rule is to err on the side of caution.

c. *Use first names for the next reporting level.* A departmental employee may address a manager by first name, but not a vice-president. This rank-by-rank system is the practice in many companies, especially larger ones.

d. *Use first names universally.* This is often the rule in smaller companies, where everything takes place informally.

e. *Base your decision on the way letters to you are signed.* Once an executive signs his or her first name, you may take that as a signal that informal style is acceptable.

f. *Decide on the basis of what others do.* Perhaps the most prudent approach is to observe. If you notice other, equally-ranked employees using the informal, you may do likewise.

g. *Ask permission.* If you are uncertain, it is preferable to ask than to assume either way.

2. The chain of command is often thought of from the bottom up. But the other side—from the top down—is equally important, and the structure should be respected in both ways. Unfortunately, that rule is not always followed. Some ideas:

a. *Ask that instructions to your subordinates be passed through your office.* This is a proper and appropriate request, but it should be made with the utmost of diplomacy.

b. *Have subordinates ask for respect for the chain of command.* When executives make demands on employees, it puts the employees' priorities in conflict; they must report to two bosses. They have the right to ask not to be placed in that position.

c. *Suggest procedures to protect subordinates from chain-of-command violations.* If the problem is severe, you may have to bring it to the attention of the company's leaders. If you do, be prepared to offer concrete and workable solutions.

d. *Deliver the completed task yourself.* A violation of the chain of command is the first wrong. Allowing a subordinate to complete the task by delivering the result only confirms and allows the violation to go unchallenged. Delivering the work yourself gives you an opportunity to clarify your role and to ask that the chain of command be respected.

e. *Present constructive solutions rather than complaints.* For example, you may point out to the executive that, by delegating the assignment, the executive will be relieved of the need to follow up.

3. In order to survive within the chain of command, you first need to define how well it works. Questions worth asking are:

   a. *How effective is the reporting structure?* If it simply isn't working, you will have to contend with the status quo. However, if it works well, you need to ensure that your subordinates understand and follow it.

   b. *How formal is the chain of command?* In some small companies, the chain of command is little more than a responsibility cycle. The titles and rank don't matter that much, so an overly formal recognition of it could become a negative. By the same argument, a highly formal reporting chain limits the actions and contacts of everyone in the organization.

   c. *Does it work in both directions?* A chain of command that applies only to those beneath someone in rank is an example of poor organization. The most desirable situation is one in which everyone—high- and low-ranking—appreciates the chain of command and follows the rules.

   d. *Does the structure grow in times of business expansion?* One danger is that during periods of growth, the complexity and size of the staff grows as well. However, when expansion stops or contraction begins, it may be more difficult to reduce the chain of command.

   e. *Are executive layers growing more rapidly than rank and file?* If so, that's a danger signal. It means that top management is trying to solve problems by increasing its "layers of caution," rather than taking the opposite step: improving communication and effectiveness on all levels.

CHAPTER 4

1. Guests are expected to respond to invitations and to behave properly during the meal. These rules apply:

   a. *Reply promptly to the invitation.* Don't delay your response.

   b. *If you do decline the invitation, give the reason.* Also propose a later appointment date and time.

   c. *Make sure you know where the meal will be held and what rules apply there.* You might not be able to consume certain foods, for example, or might not be properly dressed for a particular restaurant. Find out in advance if any of these problems will apply.

d. *Decline inappropriate invitations directly.* A proposed business meal might not be acceptable due to the time or day or because of the relationship itself.

e. *Be aware of who is controlling the agenda.* As a general rule, the person making the invitation and paying for the meal will be in control. Don't spend the meeting struggling with your host for control.

2. Business meal hosts should observe these rules:

a. *Invite others for business reasons.* Unless the other person is also a close personal friend, you should have a business agenda for the business meal.

b. *Stick to the stated agenda.* Since you invited someone else to the meeting, you owe it to the person to introduce and discuss the topic.

c. *Do not impose the idea on others.* Subordinates, for example, might assume that there is no choice involved, that they must accept your invitation. Make it clear that going to a business meal with you is not a condition of employment.

d. *Ask for a response as soon as possible.* When you extend an invitation, you deserve a prompt reply.

e. *Be aware of appearances.* If you seem to be favoring one subordinate over others in the department, it will look like favoritism, even when it is not. You may have to exercise diplomacy and invite all employees with equal frequency.

3. The question of whether or not to order an alcoholic drink is a difficult one. Ask yourself:

a. *Is there a company policy?* Your company may forbid drinking during the lunch hour. Even when there is no specific written policy, the practice might be frowned upon from the top.

b. *How much should you drink?* To be on the safe side, don't take more than one drink during a business meal.

c. *What if you are not sure?* In this case, take the safe choice: Order a nonalcoholic drink.

d. *Will you drive after the meal?* If so, you should order a nonalcoholic drink, even if you know you can handle one or two. Take the safe

route and, at the same time, make a good impression on your business associates.
  e. *Do you even want a drink?* Don't allow others to pressure you into drinking, and ignore any nonverbal sense of pressure. If you don't want a drink, you should not have one.

CHAPTER 5

1. Popular myths about promptness tie the idea in with a concept about power and influence. These myths are:
  a. *The person who keeps someone else waiting has the advantage.* This might contain an element of truth, in the sense that the individual exercises the power of holding up another employee's schedule. However, it is an extremely negative, short-term form of power that does not create a positive attitude in the corporate environment.
  b. *It is better to be late than early, since the early person admits his or her disadvantage.* Again, this myth assumes that every appointment involves the unspoken question: Which of the people has greater power and influence? Perhaps a more relevant question is: Which of the two understands basic courtesy and professional behavior?
  c. *If you show up on time, you appear to be overly precise or, perhaps, too anxious.* This places you in a weak position. In reality, being on time is admirable and is a standard worth striving for.
2. The following are rules of common courtesy regarding appointment promptness:
  a. *Being early is far better than being late.* You lose no ground by being early.
  b. *Being on time should become an important standard, one you believe exhibits an attitude of professionalism.*
  c. *If you are late for an appointment, you should explain and apologize.* While lateness is unavoidable in some cases, you should make it your personal rule never to be late intentionally.
3. Your personal appointment guidelines may include the following ideas:
  a. *Apply the same standards to everyone.* If you find yourself keeping subordinates waiting but showing up promptly for meetings with

people of higher rank, consider the statement that behavior makes. Don't allow someone else's rank and title to dictate your behavior.

b. *Adopt a customer service attitude, both externally and internally.* Most departments work with other departments, whether they interact with external customers or not. In that interaction, another department is your customer.

c. *Be more aware of good manners than of power and influence.* Your behavior should be guided by common sense and fair treatment, not by your opinion of someone's rank—either above or below yours on the chain of command.

d. *Don't allow others to keep you waiting unreasonably.* Set a standard for yourself. How many minutes represent a reasonable delay? When that point has passed, it's time to get on to other tasks. This is not a power statement, but a response to discourteous behavior.

e. *Always apologize when you are late.* Be on time unless circumstances beyond your control create a problem. Create a reputation for yourself as a dependable, professional, and responsible member of the corporate family.

CHAPTER 6

1. In some meetings, the official leader does not truly lead. You may take over the leadership position and will need to proceed cautiously. The guidelines are:

a. *Always pose your ideas for action as recommendations and never as orders.* You need to respect the official leader's title and not make it appear as though you are taking over.

b. *Ask the leader questions that will lead to conclusions you need to implement.* A good way to lead while still showing respect for the official leader is to channel ideas through that individual.

c. *Volunteer to take responsibility for follow-up actions.* Knowing that the official leader is unable to follow up as he or she should, you may need to take charge. However, rather than merely assuming power, volunteer; that gives the leader the opportunity to accept your offer.

    d. *Report through the meeting leader.* Even when you have completely taken over projects or other follow-up actions, keep the official leader involved.

    e. *Inform the meeting leader of all decisions and actions.* If, during the follow-up phase, you need to take action or make decisions, be sure to let the official leader know in advance.

2. As the leader of an internal meeting, you will succeed by following these rules:

    a. *Announce start and stop times in advance.* Let attendees know how long they will be away from their departments.

    b. *Observe the time constraints.* Make every effort to start on time whenever possible. Even when you are forced to start late, end the meeting at the announced time.

    c. *Take steps to minimize interruptions.* Use a room where you can close the door and where no traffic will distract your meeting. Also disconnect the telephone in the room while your meeting is in progress.

    d. *List agenda items in priority order.* Take care of the most important topics first. If you cannot get to the lower priorities, they can be deferred until a later meeting, without running over the scheduled time.

    e. *Distribute the agenda in advance.* Let your attendees know what will be discussed at the meeting so they can come prepared.

    f. *Set time goals for yourself for each agenda item.* Estimate the time required to discuss each topic, and try to stick to the time limitations.

    g. *Stick to the agenda, and keep the meeting on the move.* Attendees may introduce topics not on the agenda or go off on tangents. It is the leader's job to cut short those conversations and keep the meeting on the right course.

3. When you meet with someone out of town, whether the person is affiliated with your company or not, remember these important guidelines:

    a. *Keep notes.* You may need to prepare a report for management upon your return to the office, and you will need a reminder of what was said and how you responded.

    b. *If you make promises, keep them.* Make this a very high standard for yourself. As soon as you get back to the office, follow through as you promised the other person.

    c. *Remember that you represent your company.* Everything you say will be assumed to be the official position of the company, so you need to think before you speak, to represent your management accurately; and to avoid any statement that could embarrass you or your company later.

    d. *Be careful when someone fishes for information.* Be aware of what information is confidential, and always assume that anything you say in private will be repeated later. If someone asks for information you're not sure you should give out, trust your instincts and avoid replying.

CHAPTER 7

1. Employees need to be given guidelines for telephone conduct; without guidelines, methods of answering the phone and response will vary with each individual. These guidelines include:

    a. *Take complete messages.* Be sure employees write down the name of the caller, phone number, time of the call, message, and other important information. If they promise you will call back at a specific time, that should be written on the message form.

    b. *State when the call will be returned.* Your employees should be able to tell a caller when you will be available and when you will return their call.

    c. *Use the hold button carefully.* Employees should not forget that the first caller has priority. If someone must be left on hold so another incoming call can be answered, make the second contact as brief as possible. Don't allow employees to leave anyone on hold longer than one minute; if the time will extend beyond one minute, they should take a number and call back a few minutes later.

    d. *Answer the telephone professionally.* You need to write down the precise method for employees to answer their own phone, as well as someone else's line. Remember, the method of answering creates an impression about your department.

    e. *Give explanations when transferring calls to someone else.* Be sure employees understand the frustration of being transferred; if it happens too frequently, it creates an impression of bureaucracy and incompetence. Callers should be offered an explanation, as well as the name and extension of the person to whom they are being transferred, in case they are disconnected.

2. Communication without the benefit of physical presence is very difficult, because much of what we convey is nonverbal. Thus, you need to become aware of the impression you make over the phone. Try these ideas:

   a. *Ask an employee for criticism.* Staff members may be willing to listen to your side of a conversation and share their observations with you. Unpleasant tone of voice, repeated use of stock phrases, or poor speaking habits may create negative impressions on others. Find out what flaws your style has and then work to eliminate them.

   b. *Record your own voice.* Hearing yourself will teach you a great deal about the message you convey. List the speaking habits or phrases you don't like, and then concentrate on changing your pattern.

   c. *Listen to others over the phone.* When you are involved in a conversation, be aware of the other person's telephone manners and habits. Avoid the patterns that irritate or offend you.

   d. *Work to overcome flaws.* Changing habits is never easy, and you may need to take steps to help yourself. You may list the words or cliches to avoid; have an employee listen critically; or record your side of the conversation again, and listen for flaws.

3. Rules of etiquette worth observing, both for yourself and for staff members, include:

   a. *Always return phone calls.* Make it your personal standard that a caller will never need to leave more than one message.

   b. *Avoid telephone interruptions of meetings.* Don't allow the telephone to become more important than the face-to-face meeting. Respect other people's time by having calls intercepted by someone else while meetings are underway.

   c. *Listen carefully.* Give the other person your full attention, and don't try to listen while you also work on other tasks.

   d. *Screen calls honestly.* It is never necessary to lie to a caller. Being "unavailable" is general enough in any instance. However, a screen should also include a commitment as to the time a call will be returned.

e. *Use the hold button cautiously.* Remember that no one likes being left on hold. One minute should be the maximum without voice contact.

f. *Be aware of how you sound.* You need to listen to two voices during every conversation: the other person's and your own.

g. *Don't misuse answering machines.* The machine is a convenience and shouldn't be used to screen calls you don't want to take. Return every call for which a recorded message is left.

h. *Set departmental policies for answering the telephone.* Be sure employees understand exactly how you want the phone answered and how and when messages are to be returned.

CHAPTER 8

1. Rules of correspondence include:

a. *Follow accepted formats.* Once your company finds a format that works, stick with it. For memos and letters, follow traditional formats. If you want to suggest any changes, do so through the chain of command.

b. *Be aware of first impressions.* Neatness does count. Make sure all written material coming from your department meets minimum standards of neatness.

c. *Check spelling thoroughly, especially for names.* Your written communications should be carefully checked for obvious spelling errors before leaving the department. Be especially careful in the spelling of names.

d. *Edit with the goal of reduction.* A shorter, clearer message is better than a longer one. Forcing yourself to shorten a letter or memo invariably improves and clarifies your message.

e. *Write in a clear style.* Resist the tendency to try to make your message sound important. Important ideas come across when they are expressed simply and directly.

f. *Never let unacceptable material leave the department.* You can delegate the task of cross-editing and checking to your staff. Specify minimal standards, and enforce them.

2. In editing your work, remember these points:
   a. *If you're having a problem deciding how to express an idea, put it aside for a while.* Some problems are best solved by taking a break. Come back to it later, and try again.
   b. *Ask someone else to review your work.* Ask for constructive criticism, and take it.
   c. Don't put especially difficult messages in writing at all. Remember, you are not limited only to written communication. A telephone call or, better yet, a face-to-face meeting might be more appropriate for sensitive issues.
   d. *If there is a misunderstanding, ask for a face-to-face meeting.* Resolve the problem without delay. Confront the problem, explaining that you did not intend to convey the message that was received.
3. When sending copies, follow these guidelines:
   a. *Send copies to everyone mentioned in the memo or letter or whose area of responsibility will be affected.* Every department manager who is involved in the issue being discussed deserves the courtesy of a copy.
   b. *If in doubt, send a copy.* Borderline cases should always be decided in favor of the least offensive course. You are better off sending a copy unnecessarily than not sending one and creating a problem.
   c. *List the names of everyone to whom a copy was sent.* Each recipient should be informed of the names of everyone seeing the same material.
   d. *Send blind copies very selectively.* In some limited cases, you will want to send a copy of a letter or memo to someone without letting the primary recipient know. In those cases, label the copy as a "blind" copy.

CHAPTER 9

1. Even on a limited budget, you can still dress properly in the organization. Some ideas:
   a. *Seek well-tailored but affordable clothing.* Take the time to compare prices.

    b. *Buy on a payment plan.* Going into debt for your professional wardrobe, as long as you remain in control of its level, is a sound investment.

    c. *Build your wardrobe gradually over time.* You probably don't need to completely replace the entire wardrobe all at once.

    d. *Add variety with well-planned and tasteful accessories.*

2. Dress according to the unspoken rules, remembering that the rules don't apply everywhere:

    a. *Be aware of regional customs.* What works in New York might not work in Hawaii.

    b. *The rules may change with the season.* Don't base your entire wardrobe on the way others dress at a specific time of the year. Be aware of how the rules change with the weather.

    c. *Personal appearance and body type may limit the way you can dress or may provide opportunities for more variety.* Coordinate your own style with your personal appearance.

    d. *Work within your budget.* Don't spend more than you can afford, either for cash purchase or by going deeply into debt for business clothing.

3. You can get good fashion ideas from a number of sources. Some ideas:

    a. *Your best learning tool is the eye.* Watch what others wear. What is pleasing, and what is distracting?

    b. *Many stores offer the services of a fashion consultant.* If not, shop where salespeople know their merchandise and are willing to devote time to work with you in selecting the best possible wardrobe.

    c. *Check business magazines, especially the ads.* That's one of the best places to find out what is current and eye-pleasing.

    d. *Ask friends and business peers for advice, especially those whose fashion sense you admire.*

CHAPTER 10

1. Newly-hired managers need to observe special rules of behavior, including:

    a. *Keep a low profile.* Wait until you know your way around the culture before taking a stand. Avoid being disruptive until you understand the political and social rules.

b. *Consolidate your position slowly.* There is no rush to get "up to speed." Avoid creating problems for yourself by trying to make your mark too quickly.

c. *Ask a lot of questions.* For new managers, questions are more important than answers. Your job for the first month or two on the job is knowing which questions to ask.

d. *Learn the unspoken rules.* Every company observes its own special rules, which you will discover in one of two ways: by making mistakes or by quietly observing.

e. *Suggest improvements, but proceed cautiously.* You may see room for positive change, but you will improve your chances for success by getting staff members on your side before mentioning your ideas for change. Employ tact, and listen to staff ideas.

2. Until you have been on the job long enough to be thought of as a member of the corporate family, speak out only in these circumstances:

a. *To obtain information on procedures or rules.* Curiosity is the new manager's most admirable attribute. Wisdom comes later.

b. *To communicate in both directions.* Your staff will be apprehensive until it knows you better, so communication may be difficult at first. You ease this situation by demonstrating good listening skills.

c. *To suggest ideas cautiously.* You may see an obvious way to improve immediately the way things are being done. However, if you can get an employee responsible for the procedure to suggest the change or at least to endorse your idea enthusiastically, the change will be far less threatening to staff members.

d. *To solve employee problems.* Newly-hired managers may inherit a range of personal problems and conflicts. Open the doors of communication, whether the conflict exists between two subordinates or between your department and another.

3. Job transfers within the same company can be delicate political events. Remember these rules:

a. *Tell your current boss.* Give supervisors the time they will need to replace you. You may ignore this rule only if your relationship with your supervisor is poor and that's the main reason you're seeking a transfer, in which case, sharing this information could backfire.

b. *Make the application through proper channels.* If you company posts new jobs, apply in conformity with company policy. Don't try to circumvent the procedure by going directly to the supervisor in the other division.

c. *Suggest a transitional training period.* Make yourself available to complete ongoing projects, work with your replacement, and provide any other help that might be needed to effect a smooth transition.

CHAPTER 11

1. Turning negative messages into positive ones takes practice but is not difficult. For example:
   a. Negative: No one understands what I have to put up with.
      Positive: I'd like to explain my priorities, so that you'll understand my point of view.
   b. Negative: Why do I always get the big problems?
      Positive: We operate under considerable pressure, as I'm sure you do.
   c. Negative: Why can't you take care of this without bothering me?
      Positive: I'd like you to work with me in arriving at a solution.
   d. Negative: This isn't my problem.
      Positive: How would you solve this problem?

2. Bringing the question of profit into a complaint, especially when you are communicating with your company's decision makers, leads to better response. For example:
   a. You could complain about inadequate floor space, complaining, "You let that other department expand. I want more space, too." Or, in a more positive vein, you could say, "I've noticed a drop in quality and efficiency since we became so crowded. Here's a report estimating the dollar cost to the company. . . ."
   b. A broken photocopy machine is frustrating and inconvenient, but it also costs the company a lot of money. You may complain, "We need a machine that isn't always breaking down at the worst

time." Or you could research replacement costs, include a summary of maintenance expenses for the last year, and add in the expense of staff idle time, then make a case for reducing expenses by buying a new model.

c. Administrative duties may take up much of your time, but bringing the problem to your boss won't solve the problem. You may offer a solution, however: "I know how much time I spend ordering supplies, and I assume every other manager does likewise. I recommend we centralize the procedure and create a department to order for the whole company. That would save time and allow us also to take advantage of volume discounts."

3. Complaining can become a powerful communication and influence tool, if you follow these steps:

a. *Educate yourself.* Before expressing the complaint, find out what pressures the other side lives with.

b. *Look at the problem from the broadest possible perspective.* Keep the company's objectives in mind, and be aware of the issue beyond the departmental point of view.

c. *Express complaints in terms of solutions.* Avoid delegating your problems to your boss; instead, develop one or more solutions, and take that to the discussion.

CHAPTER 12

1. A popular belief states that showing up early for an appointment is a sign of weakness and that being late—or later than the other person—gives you the advantage. If you are right on time, the belief goes, you're overly anxious or too organized. In truth, though, showing up on time demonstrates a professional attitude and sends the message that you respect the other person's time.

2. Employees learn the promptness ethic when you follow these standards:

a. *Be prompt yourself.* You cannot expect others to obey your rules until you're able to follow them yourself. Show employees that you respect their time by beginning meetings and appointments in your department at the time stated.

b. *Expect promptness from staff, and say as much.* The employee who shows up for work every morning at the right time without fail may also be chronically late for meetings during the day. You need to set rules *and* to communicate those rules to staff.

c. *Train employees to set immediate goals tied to the clock.* Many people are not in the habit of setting and reaching goals. You can teach this method while setting the standard that promptness does count.

d. *Don't vary your standard based on rank.* Apply the same rules of courtesy to all others. This demonstrates your respect to staff members, even when they are entry-level.

3. Some people, including experienced executives, may never become aware of the importance of time etiquette. In that situation, you may need to take these steps:

a. *Communicate in terms of time constraints.* Let the executive know you have other appointments and priorities to execute after the meeting (a specific time is desirable) or that you need information by a specific day in order to meet deadlines.

b. *Check again before your deadline.* The disorganized executive will need to be reminded—perhaps more than once. Diplomatically confirm promises made or appointments set previously.

c. *Organize for the executive.* You can train other people to become organized by the example you set or by gently offering a suggestion that helps. This also solves a problem for the executive, which is an extra benefit to the strategy.

Index